THRIVING WITH AUTISM

90 Activities
to Encourage Your Child's
Communication,
Engagement, and Play

KATIE COOK, MED, BCBA

Illustrations by Cleonique Hilsaca

ROCKRIDGE
PRESS

For my loving mother, Robin Paulsen O'Neil, PhD, who was both a superb researcher and brilliant writer. Her uniquely steadfast integrity and eternal kindness inspired me to be the best person I can be. For my father, Kelly James O'Neil, MD, whose love, encouragement, and examples of success and passion for life bestowed upon me the strength and ambition to take on any challenge.

Interior and Cover Designer: Regina Stadnik
Art Producer: Sue Bischofberger
Editor: Seth Schwartz
Production Manager: Oriana Siska
Production Editor: Ruth Sakata Corley

Illustration © 2020 Cleonique Hilsaca

ISBN: Print 978-1-64611-480-1
eBook 978-1-64611-481-8

R1

CONTENTS

INTRODUCTION

Hello and welcome to *Thriving with Autism.*

Before getting started on this fun-filled journey together, I'd like to introduce myself. I've dedicated my career to helping children with autism find success and happiness in their lives. I'm a Board Certified Behavior Analyst, which means I've spent years learning about how behavior and learning take place. In addition, my master's degree is in teaching with a concentration in educating children with autism. I'm passionate about supporting parents in their journey to teach and lovingly connect with their children by providing training on evidence-based practices for children with autism and practical advice that's both fun and easy for caregivers to implement. I have over a decade of experience teaching children with autism and providing parent training.

Part 1 of this book (chapters 1 and 2) describes an empowering approach to teaching children with autism. It's called Applied Behavior Analysis, and I'll explain how to get the most from this therapy. In the second part of the book, you'll jump into activities proven to help your child build on essential skills and gain new ones, too. When you wholeheartedly engage in these activities, you'll achieve great outcomes for your child.

In chapter 1, I'll give you a brief overview of Autism Spectrum Disorder (ASD), Applied Behavior Analysis (ABA), and additional intervention options. I'll delve into the truth behind what autism is and is not, taking a compassionate look at what makes a child with ASD unique and what developmental challenges a child with autism will likely face. I'll answer important questions about ABA to ensure you understand the strong research and scientific evidence supporting this therapy before you begin this special teaching journey with your child. I'll also encourage you to discover your role as a parent of a child with special needs and give you a variety of strategies to take care of yourself—because you are truly the most important person in your child's life.

In chapter 2, you'll get an overview of the specific activity topics in this book: communication, engagement, play, social skills, motor movement, sensory integration, self-regulation, academics, and self-help skills. I'll also explain the purpose of the activities provided and show you how to use this book successfully when teaching your child these different skills.

Part 2 (chapters 3 to 11) is devoted to providing you with an extensive variety of playful games and activities you can do with your child to teach essential skills. Each chapter starts with an overview of why the particular skill set may be significant for your child. And in each chapter, you'll find 10 activities, based on the science of ABA, to help your child grow in each skill area.

One difference you will notice in this book, compared to most parenting resources, is that I want you to have fun while teaching your child. You will enjoy the precious moments you have dedicated to this educational time with your child, and your relationship will be strengthened through delightful experiences together. Additionally, your child will take pleasure in learning with you, which often increases how quickly a new skill is acquired. Using the activities and tips in the following chapters will create new, exciting learning opportunities for your child. We are going to work together to help your child succeed by combining my clinical experience and expertise with your enthusiasm and love for your child. I know you will accomplish your goal of helping your child thrive!

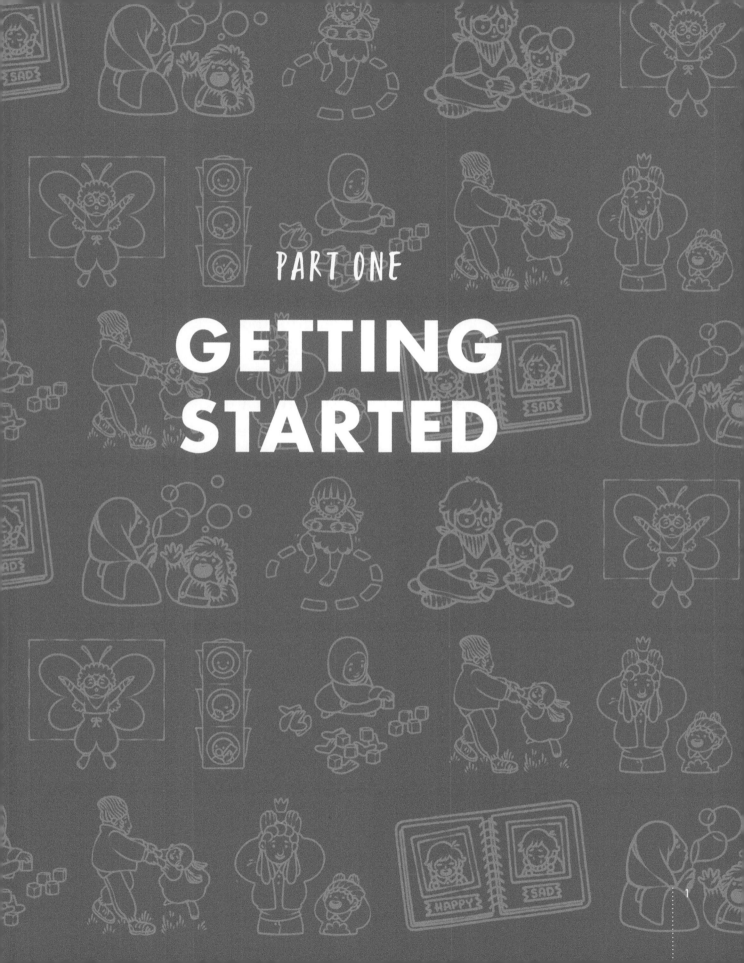

PART ONE

GETTING STARTED

CHAPTER 1

AN EMPOWERING APPROACH

Autism is a spectrum disorder, meaning children diagnosed with ASD will have a large range of strengths and weaknesses in their social skills, communication, sensory processing, academic abilities, and self-regulation. For example, although some researchers estimate that one-third of people with autism are nonverbal, many children with autism are highly verbal and have vocabulary skills well beyond their age. "If you've met one person with autism, you've met one person with autism." This quote by Dr. Stephen Shore, a special-education professional and autism advocate diagnosed with ASD, perfectly demonstrates the broad diversity among those on the autism spectrum.

There are many different therapies and techniques to choose from to help children with ASD strengthen their skills. When looking deeper into these autism therapies, you'll find significant differences in the amount of scientific evidence supporting the effectiveness of each therapy. In this book, I'll primarily focus on ABA, one therapy approach with a tremendous amount of scientific evidence proving its effectiveness treating children diagnosed with autism.

WHAT IS APPLIED BEHAVIOR ANALYSIS?

Applied Behavior Analysis (ABA) is a therapy that applies the scientific principles of behavior to increase important social behavior and decrease behavior that may be negatively affecting a person's life. The definition of "behavior" is anything a person says or does. This means there are some behaviors we want to see our children do more often, and some behaviors we'd like to see our children do less often. In this book, I'll focus on the behaviors you'd like to see your children do more often. These behaviors are often called "skills." ABA therapy consists of many effective methods to strengthen weak skills and also teach new, appropriate skills.

All the techniques I describe in the activities in this book rely on *positive reinforcement.* Positive reinforcement occurs when the consequence that follows a behavior increases the likelihood that the behavior will occur again in the future. Here's a scenario to help you understand this important concept:

Imagine a child says the word "popcorn," and as a result they're given a piece of popcorn. If in the future the child begins to say the word "popcorn" more often, positive reinforcement has taken place. Saying the word "popcorn" is the behavior that's been strengthened, and the positive reinforcement is the actual popcorn given to the child.

Professional ABA therapy most often takes place in a one-on-one session inside a child's home. ABA therapy is also sometimes provided at a child's school or in a clinic setting. A typical ABA therapy session runs for two to three hours. Most children diagnosed with ASD receive ABA therapy multiple days each week. Depending on the child's needs, the total number of therapy hours can range from five to forty hours per week. Many children diagnosed with ASD will receive ABA for much of their childhood, starting therapy as toddlers and continuing into high school.

During ABA therapy, a behavior practitioner works directly with a child, implementing proven learning strategies for children with autism. Effective modern ABA techniques are designed to be very enjoyable for the child. In fact, most ABA therapy programs begin with a phase that's intended for the child to connect the behavior practitioner with rewards and positive things before any skills are taught. Most ABA therapy programs are designed and supervised by a Board Certified Behavior Analyst (BCBA) who has studied and practiced implementing the principles of behavior for many years.

How Does It Work?

ABA is an effective therapy for teaching new skills and strengthening *socially significant behaviors.* Socially significant behaviors are those that will help an individual have a more meaningful and fulfilling life. For a child with autism, these skills might include the ability to make new friends, communicate with family members, and get ready for school independently.

The science of behavior is based on one central principle: What happens after a behavior occurs will determine whether that behavior will happen again in the future and how often it will happen. Put simply, if a behavior is followed by something pleasing, the person will do that behavior more often. And if a behavior is not followed by something pleasant, that behavior will likely happen less often. If a child is doing something often, then something the child enjoys is happening after the behavior occurs. Understanding

the science of behavior helps you understand why your child behaves the way they do. You can take advantage of the principle of positive reinforcement to change what behaviors or skills your child displays.

When using ABA to help a child acquire new behavior patterns or strengthen current skills, all strategies include the use of reinforcement. This is because human behavior only happens repeatedly when it's followed by reinforcement. In the very first ABA programs, clinicians sometimes used punishment to decrease challenging behavior. Modern ABA therapy programs no longer find these methods acceptable practice. In fact, *positive reinforcement* is the foundation of ABA therapy. Most parents are very happy to learn this. Using ABA strategies is a great way to teach children because they'll likely have a wonderful time learning and enjoy the rewards and feedback they get throughout the activity!

When implementing ABA, it's important to make sure the child is able to do the skill we'd like to reinforce. *Prompting* is the process of helping the child enough so they can display the desired new skill. Prompting can be done in a variety of ways. For example, caregivers can model the desired behavior, showing the child exactly what to do by doing it first. Other prompting methods include gesturing to the right answer or physically assisting a child to display the correct response. Once a child receives the ideal amount of prompting assistance, they'll be able to demonstrate the skill correctly. This is when the child's instructor will immediately provide reinforcement to increase the likelihood that the child will be able to display the newly learned skill again in the future. This process is repeated until the child reaches independence with the skill, and prompting is no longer necessary.

Why Use Applied Behavior Analysis?

ABA is the gold standard for helping children with autism reach their full potential. More than four decades of scientific research support the effectiveness of ABA-based procedures to increase appropriate skills for children with autism. In addition, the US Surgeon General and the American Psychological Association consider ABA an evidence-based best practice treatment. This is important because it means the interventions used in ABA have been proven with scientific evidence to help children with autism. Some of the evidence-based practices (EBPs) for children with ASD explained in this book are positive reinforcement, functional communication training, modeling, naturalistic teaching, peer-mediated instruction, prompting, scripting, social narratives, social skills training, task analysis, video modeling, and visual supports.

Parents and clinicians agree there are many reasons that ABA empowers children to develop needed skills and reach their highest potential. ABA focuses on foundational and everyday skills. ABA programs target communication skills (requesting, asking questions, holding a conversation), social/emotional skills (greetings, initiating friendships, body language), and adaptive life skills (toileting, brushing teeth, getting dressed). Furthermore, one of the basic philosophical values of most ABA therapeutic programs is that individuals with ASD have the right to the least restrictive treatment possible. This means that, when implementing ABA strategies, we attempt to help the child make the largest gains possible while minimizing potential distress. ABA treatment is individualized to each learner while holding to the central assumption that everyone with autism is capable of learning. Goals are selected and prioritized by their highest likelihood of making significant positive changes to the child's life. ABA is not a one-size-fits-all approach to teaching. ABA is exceptionally successful in helping children with autism in large part because the behavior clinician chooses and modifies strategies to meet the unique needs of each individual learner.

COMPLEMENTARY THERAPIES

Most professionals agree there is no singular autism therapy. Several therapies other than ABA have shown positive outcomes in treating specific symptoms of autism.

Occupational therapy. Occupational therapy practitioners often work with children in the areas of play skills, motor skills, and self-care. For example, occupational therapists implement strategies intended to teach skills such as coloring, writing, cutting with scissors, walking, running, climbing, jumping, grooming, eating, and dressing. Occupational therapy can be conducted at a child's school, in the home, or at a therapist's office. It can be delivered to a child one-on-one or in a group setting. The overarching purpose of occupational therapy is to improve fine and gross motor skills and motor planning.

Speech-language therapy. The objective of speech-language therapy is to increase a child's speech and language skills. Children are taught to use vocal language, sign language, or augmentative and alternative communication (AAC) devices. Some common goals of speech-language therapy include word articulation, conversation skills, nonverbal communication, and social skills. This therapy can be delivered to a child one-on-one or in a group setting. Speech-language therapy sessions generally occur at a child's school or in a clinic setting.

Sensory integration therapy. Sensory integration therapies aim to improve a child's atypical response to common stimuli, such as household sounds, smells, and textures. Symptoms of autism often include sensory processing difficulties. Sounds, smells, and even textures can affect a child with autism in a unique way. The world around them can become overwhelming and uncomfortable. Therapy usually includes developing a sensory diet—a routine of scheduled activities that expose the child to a variety of sensory input.

Play therapy. Play therapy primarily focuses on increasing symbolic play and communication skills. Children with autism often play in a way noticeably different from how typical children play. Also called *floor time*, play therapy is conducted on the floor with toys and games. Play therapy sessions are designed to create opportunities to practice communication skills during enjoyable activities. An adult encourages the development of symbolic play for the child by modeling imaginary play and appropriate engagement with toys.

WHAT'S MY ROLE AS A PARENT?

As you discover your role as a parent to a child diagnosed with ASD, you may find it helpful to identify your views on parenting in general. Although individual parenting styles vary from family to family, many caregivers describe their primary role as being their child's first and most important teacher. This teacher role continues throughout all the developmental stages of your child's life. You're also your child's most consistent teacher. The bonds and trust you have with your child are unparalleled. You have the opportunity to expose your child to more age-appropriate challenges and learning moments than any other adult in your child's life.

Your role as teacher to your child with autism will expand as you become more educated in the precise strategies established to be effective with your child. Proven ABA techniques equip you with the teaching strategies to be the most valuable teacher in your child's life. Parents and caregivers of children diagnosed with autism are essential to a child's success with ABA-based therapies. Empowered parents take an active role in their child's ABA programs. This means learning all you can about the evidence-based practices of ABA and implementing these strategies as fully as possible within your household.

Parent training in ABA is the cornerstone for successful outcomes for children with autism. Numerous studies have shown that parent training is a very effective method for promoting acquisition, generalization, and maintenance of skills in children with autism. Parents participating in ABA therapy programs are always trained to implement treatment techniques to ensure that their effects are maintained even after ABA therapy sessions have ended. Reading about evidence-based practices for autism, such as the ones described in this book, is a terrific way to start the journey to become the most valuable teacher in your child's life.

Here are 10 tips for being your child's most valuable teacher:

- Educate yourself about effective teaching strategies. (You'll find resources at the end of this book.)
- Learn about the medical diagnosis of autism and the personal experiences of individuals diagnosed with autism.
- Shine a spotlight on all your child's strengths, and share compliments with your child and the professionals and caregivers surrounding them.
- Focus on your child's interests. Teach your child as many skills as possible while engaging in their favorite activities.
- Keep learning settings and materials organized and clutter-free to minimize distractions.
- Create and maintain schedules and routines to make tasks and learning easier for your child.

- Reinforce appropriate behavior. Use positive reinforcement in the form of rewards and praise to keep your child motivated to learn with you.
- Practice skills in a variety of settings with multiple people.
- Use different types of materials to practice skills.
- Keep teaching. No one can predict how quickly your child will learn needed skills.

CARING FOR THE CAREGIVER

Parenting can be blissful and overwhelming at the same time. As a parent, you wear a lot of hats: caregiver, provider, chef, teacher, counselor, information specialist, and more. This role grows tenfold when you're a parent to a child with autism. Parents of children with autism must navigate a world that bombards them with information about what they should and shouldn't do to help their child succeed. Raising an autistic child can be exceptionally difficult for a parent and requires increased patience and self-control. Studies show that parents of a child with ASD have greater levels of stress, anxiety, and depression compared to the rest of the population.

Your emotional health is critical to your child's well-being and developmental progress. When you're able to meet your emotional and physical needs, your child will benefit, too. It's crucial that you make time for yourself and develop coping strategies. Try to implement these self-care routines:

- Obtain support from other parents. Contact your local autism society or nonprofit organization to join parenting group meetings online or in your local community.
- Lean on your friends. Let them give you emotional support or hands-on help by providing you with breaks, babysitting, or taking on other tasks when they offer. Don't be afraid to ask your friends for specific help. They often have a deep desire to support you and just don't know how.
- Maintain your physical health. Get to your medical appointments and follow your physician's instructions and treatment plans to ensure you stay physically healthy.
- Set boundaries. Be mindful not to agree to meetings, tasks, or responsibilities that you're aware may push your stress levels too high. It's okay to say no when necessary, even to the professionals in your child's life.
- Use calming strategies. Get regular exercise, meditate on happy thoughts, stop and take deep breaths, journal positive outcomes and gratitude, listen to music, relax with aromatherapy, fuel your body with healthy food, and practice yoga stretches.

CHAPTER 2

ENGAGE, CONNECT, AND THRIVE

This book endeavors to open a beautiful new chapter in the life you and your child share by giving you practical ABA strategies to engage and connect with each other. Being involved with your child's ABA therapy allows you to be a leader in building foundational, everyday skills to help your child thrive. Using ABA interventions is one of the most important ways to reach your child at the deepest levels. ABA therapy helps you transcend the barriers of autism. You'll use ABA to teach your child vital communication and social skills and a variety of life skills your child needs to thrive in a way you may never have thought possible.

WHAT'S AHEAD FOR YOU IN THE BOOK?

The remaining chapters in this book focus on these selected skill areas because of the significant impact they'll have on your child's life:

COMMUNICATION SKILLS are necessary for your child to get their wants and needs met every day. One that caregivers can teach using the activities in the book is the essential skill of making requests. In the activity Bubbles, Bubbles, Glorious Bubbles (page 22), you will teach your child how to make requests while playing with bubbles. I will outline how to use this fun activity to increase your child's language and ability to make requests, whether your child is nonverbal or learning to use full sentences. In the activity Chocolate Time (page 31), your child will practice describing what is happening in their environment while creating a delicious beverage with you. The steps and tips on how to make this fun activity effective in increasing your child's language are provided, and you will enjoy taking a traditional household task and turning it into a delightful and effective opportunity for your child to strengthen their communication skills.

ENGAGEMENT SKILLS allow your child to take advantage of developmental growth opportunities in their everyday life. Engagement is taught in many of the activities that focus on increasing your child's ability to share joint attention with someone else. In the activity One Little Finger (page 36), your child will learn the important skill of joint attention while performing hand gestures and singing along with you to a short, amusing song. In the activity Funny Features (page 40), you will help your child expand their perspective beyond the concrete and literal meaning of words and strengthen their flexibility of mind. Over time, playing silly games like this one will help your child connect with others by increasing their awareness of the feelings and thoughts of other people around them.

PLAY SKILLS give your child the ability to learn in an entertaining way while also strengthening the friendships in their life.

Vital play skills that can be taught using the activities in this book include parallel play, pretend play, and cooperative play, just to name a few. Participating in the Magic Box (page 50) activity will strengthen your child's pretend play skills while you help them turn ordinary household items into amusing new toys. In the activity Beautiful Friendships (page 55), I will give you useful tips on how to host a successful playdate for your child. Within this activity, you will learn everything you need to know to increase your child's parallel and associative play skills when playing with a peer.

SOCIAL SKILLS allow your child to engage in rewarding relationships and create lifelong friendships. An example of a social skill that can be strengthened using the activities in this book is eye contact. A fun activity to teach eye contact is Face Painting (page 69). I will give you the recipe for homemade face paint and the shortcuts needed to enjoy a brief face-painting activity at home with your child that is designed to increase eye contact and your connection to one another. In the activity The Listening High Five (page 67), you and your child will complete a simple art project created to teach your child how to be a good active listener.

MOTOR SKILLS are the movements of your child's body and allow your child to physically interact in the world around them. Examples of motor skills that can be strengthened using the activities are holding a pencil to write and throwing a ball. The Raisin Race (page 87) activity combines the excitement of competition with the pleasure of healthy snacks to strengthen your child's fine motor skills. In Balancing Bonanza (page 89), two or three players take turns performing zany physical actions that strengthen multiple muscles at a time. Both gross motor and balancing skills are increased while playing this entertaining indoor game.

SENSORY INTEGRATION is your child's ability to sense the world around them, including how they see, feel, and hear things. Improved sensory integration will make your child feel more physically comfortable when coming into contact with stimuli in their environment, like noise, wind, and bright lights. In the activity The Human Burrito (page 96), you and your child will have loads of fun playing on the floor with blankets, pillows, and other household items. By following the steps in this activity, you will not only appreciate laughing and connecting with your child, but you will also be helping them regulate their autonomic nervous system. Other fun activities designed to increase sensory integration include clay play, freeze dancing, yoga poses, and much more.

SELF-REGULATION SKILLS offer your child a set of valuable tools to navigate and overcome the difficult and uncomfortable situations they'll almost certainly encounter throughout life. As you play the games in the chapters ahead, your child will gain a wide range of self-regulation skills, including a variety of calming strategies and self-soothing techniques. In the activity Helping Hand (page 114), self-regulation is taught through role-playing practical solutions to common frustrating situations and reading social stories that demonstrate problem-solving strategies. Using the social script provided in this activity will allow you to teach your child valuable functional communication and problem-solving skills in a comfortable and relaxed setting. Roaring Lion (page 115) is a relaxing activity that will teach you and your child a variety of breathing techniques that will calm the body.

ACADEMIC SKILLS open new doors of opportunity in your child's future. You can teach many academic skills to your child with these activities, including mathematics, reading, writing, and paying attention to a teacher. Slap Match (page 133), an adaptable two-player game, can be modified to teach academic skills from numbers and letters to historical facts. In the activity Feel and Learn (page 137), you and your child will use crafting materials, such as pipe cleaners, buttons, or pom-poms, to create art while increasing your child's academic skills. This type of learning is sometimes called tactile learning and offers an entertaining and effective way for your child to build academic skill sets.

SELF-HELP SKILLS are the key to your child's future independence. You'll learn many fun ways to teach your child valuable skills, such as using the bathroom, washing hands, getting dressed, brushing teeth, telling time, and using money. In the activity Brushy Brush Brush (page 145), I will show you how to use one of the most popular tools in ABA: the sticker chart. While brushing teeth is the main focus of this activity, you will learn how to teach your child a variety of self-help skills using this treasured positive reinforcement system. Let's Go Shopping (page 152) will take you step by step through how to have a successful community outing with your child. This activity focuses primarily on increasing your child's appropriate behavior while in a grocery store, but the tips provided will allow you to enhance the positive experiences your family has while visiting a variety of community settings.

Each chapter includes 10 different activities to teach your child specific skills. The fun and unique teaching methods are designed specifically to guide you through a game or enjoyable task that you can do with your child to teach a new skill. Within each chapter, activities are

ordered by the suggested age range of the child who is most likely to be capable of and enjoy engaging in the activity. Chapters begin with activities for children as young as one year old and gradually move through more challenging tasks for children as old as twelve.

The activities at the beginning of each chapter typically involve a lot of assistance by the caregiver and require very little language from the child. The activities provided later in the chapter require a child to independently participate in the activity and sometimes communicate using full sentences and more complicated language.

Keep in mind that the recommended ages pertain to your child's developmental age (or level) in that particular skill area. This means, for example, that if your child is currently able to communicate at the developmental level that is typical for a three-year-old, you'll want to consider activities indicated for the age of three.

Many of the activities are short enough to read in just a few minutes and to implement at home the same day. Sometimes parents have only a limited amount of time to engage with their child in a meaningful way to teach these important foundational skills. I encourage you to dip in and out of chapters as they relate to your child. You don't have to read the activities in a linear fashion. In fact, I recommend you browse through the chapters and choose to read about and complete activities that you know relate to skills that are a challenge for your child. Also, pick activities designed for your child's developmental age in that skill area. Keep in mind that you may only want to read one or two activities before choosing to try one out. You can then pick up this book again on another day and read a few more activities to select the best activity for that day.

READY TO GET STARTED?

You're about to embark on a special journey with your child. You can adjust the following activities to fit the life you've created for your family. And you can invite friends, other caregivers, and family members to join this wonderful expedition as you teach your child while having fun together.

Now is a good time to read through a few of the activities in a skill area you feel is one of the most important for your child, and then go for it! In this book, you'll find fun, active, and engaging activities designed to help you teach your child the vital skills they need to thrive. I wish both you and your child incredible success in this enjoyable bonding experience!

PART TWO

LET'S DO THIS!

Activities, Games, and Strategies

CHAPTER 3

LET'S COMMUNICATE!

As a parent of a child with autism, you've likely watched your child hit barriers that prevent full engagement in their life and with the people around them. Teaching your child to communicate at peer levels is probably the central goal you hope to accomplish with the activities in this book.

Delays in communication cause children to struggle with developing friendships, connecting with loved ones, and getting their personal needs and wants met. A child's inability to communicate effectively often leads to the display of challenging or inappropriate behaviors. These negative behaviors sometimes take the form of tantrums, aggression, or self-stimulation and are frequently the result of the frustration a child feels when they're unable to get their needs met or communicate the feelings trapped inside them. For example, if at the park a nonverbal child with autism wants to have a turn on the swing, they may begin to scream and cry in front of the swing set until an adult lifts them into the swing. The child may often scream at the park because sometimes the outburst results in being lifted into the swing. But more frequently the people around the child don't understand what they want when they scream, and they remove them from the park. This child will be able to get their desires met much more effectively once they learn to use the word "up" to ask to be lifted into the swing.

In another example, a child with autism and limited language abilities might push peers in order to get one to chase them. The child pushes peers because one of the playmates may do exactly as "requested" by chasing them around the playground. Unfortunately, most of the other peers will likely avoid being near this child on the playground to avoid being pushed. This child will be able to get their needs met and have a more enjoyable recess once they learn how to ask friends to play by vocalizing a full sentence or using the words "chase me."

Imagine how frustrating it would be to want something so much or experience extreme anxiety in a particular setting or situation but not have the power to communicate these feelings. Now, imagine how liberating it would be for your child to have the ability to use words or nonverbal communication to share their wishes. Working on communication skills with your child can give them this incredibly valuable gift.

The activities in this chapter are designed to improve your child's communication skills and alleviate the discomfort they may feel when not being able to express themselves or engage in meaningful connections with others. By participating in these fun games and activities, your child can greatly improvement their communication skills, and you'll see the positive changes that follow.

GIVING MEANING TO SOUNDS

1 Year – 4 Years

WHAT YOU'LL NEED: nothing needed for this activity.

On those days when your child seems to be in their own world, it can feel painstakingly difficult to draw them out. Maybe they have found something to fixate on, are indulging in a self-stimulatory behavior, or are peering out the window, watching the world go by. If at these times you can align yourself with what your child is doing, in some cases even engaging in the repetitive behavior they may be performing, you'll create a unique opportunity to slowly bring your child back into your world. If you're connected to your child, and engaging in their world, you'll then be able to shape actions and verbalizations into something more meaningful.

For instance, if your child is hand flapping, you can stand next to them and do the same, eventually forming the flapping into the wings of a bird, encouraging your child to soar with you around the room. Even better, if they make any sort of sounds or attempts at blending sounds at this time, you can help them realize that their sounds are important by pairing the sound with an object or action. For instance, if your child is saying "ka-ka-ka," bring them a ball and say, "Oh, did you say kick?" or "Do you want to kick this ball?" Then, demonstrate kicking or assist them in kicking the ball.

Another example of shaping your child's behavior into meaningful communication would be if your child makes the sound "dadada." Then you may say, "Did you want to dance with me? Let's dance!" In addition to shaping their behavior, this will show your child you're aware of what they're doing, value what they have to say, and are happy to be their communication partner. Imagine your child's delight when they realize for the first time that, in you, they have a communication companion!

WHY THIS ACTIVITY WORKS

It often takes children with autism some time before they find their voice and realize just how important it is to communicate with others in meaningful ways. This activity is designed help foster the connection between you and your child. It will also teach your child that communicating using words helps to fulfill needs and wants. Children who are currently able to make sounds and children on the cusp of developing their ability to speak will benefit greatly from these playful activities.

FUN WITH FOOD

2 Years – 5 Years

WHAT YOU'LL NEED: a variety of small snacks (cookie, nut or seed butter, cereal, lollipop) and a straw.

Here are a few fun activities that will increase your child's language clarity and ability to articulate sounds:

TONGUE STRENGTHENING: Put a tiny bit of peanut butter or another sticky, gooey food on the roof of your child's mouth and have them suck it off with their tongue. This helps with speech development and swallowing for children who have sensory issues with certain foods. (Afterward, focus on saying words with sounds that require the tongue to touch the roof of the mouth, such as "d" and "n.")

TONGUE TIP ELEVATION: Place a piece of cereal on the roof of your child's mouth directly behind the front teeth and ask them to hold it there for as long as they can. (Afterward, have them try saying words using sounds made with the tongue tip touching right behind the top teeth, such as "l" and "t.")

TONGUE MOVEMENT: Rub a lollipop around on your child's lips, getting them extra sticky, and then ask them to lick it all off. This is great practice moving their tongue and learning how to clean food off the exterior of their mouth. (Afterward, practice saying words with sounds using tongue protrusion, such as "th.")

MOUTH MUSCLES: Have your child drink from a straw, increasing the thickness of the beverage as their mouth muscles strengthen. (Afterward, work on words with the sound needed to pull their tongue back into their mouth, such as "d," "g," "k," and "ng.")

FACIAL TONING: "Cookie Race" is a game played while your child is lying flat on their back. Place a cookie on their forehead and challenge them to get the cookie into their mouth while moving only their face muscles. This game is super fun; it's also a good one to demonstrate before playing.

WHY THIS ACTIVITY WORKS
Poor articulation of sounds often hinders a child's ability to speak. Strengthening your child's oral motor muscles will enhance their ability to speak clearly and articulate sounds.

BUBBLES, BUBBLES, GLORIOUS BUBBLES

2 Years – 6 Years

WHAT YOU'LL NEED: a bottle of bubbles, or homemade bubbles and homemade wand (straw, pipe cleaner, sieve).

Who doesn't love watching a liquid turn into seemingly magical, iridescent balls of floating air that disappear into the sky? Bubbles are particularly intriguing to young children with autism.

So, you know you've got a captive audience when bubbles are around, and this is the first crucial factor. What's also great about bubbles is that they're the kind of toy young children need assistance to play with. Unscrewing the container of bubbles and blowing a sustainable bubble are difficult tasks for a young child to do by

themselves. This means they'll need you to help them. Take full advantage of this by eliciting as much verbal and nonverbal language as you can.

Motivate your child to ask for more bubbles. Blow a few rounds of bubbles, then stop, leaving the wand in the container. See if you can get your child to ask you to take the wand out. Then put the wand up to your mouth, but don't blow. See if you can get your child to ask you to blow. If your child is a young, early learner, you may accept them reaching for the container or wand as a way of communicating their wants, or maybe a simple initial sound, such as "ba" for "blow," is developmentally appropriate

for them. If your child has more language ability, you can elicit the sentence "Please blow more bubbles."

Motivate your child to comment about bubble play. Demonstrate commenting during play, then stop and point at a bubble with an excited look on your face and see if your child will make a comment on their own. You can give a younger child a sentence to fill in, such as "That bubble is ____." You can help a child with more language ability communicate longer, more descriptive sentences.

WHY THIS ACTIVITY WORKS

Teaching the vital communication skill of requesting first requires capturing your child's desires. Once your child is strongly motivated to have something, they're much more likely to imitate the words you're demonstrating and eventually learn to make requests on their own.

TIP To perform this activity all you'll need is a container of bubbles and a bubble wand. But don't worry if you don't have bubbles on hand. You can easily make your own with household items. All you need to do is mix one part dish soap to three parts water, add a few teaspoons of sugar, and stir. The sugar is a must, as it makes the bubbles last longer in the air. Wands can be made using anything with a hole in it, such as pipe cleaners, drinking straws, and even a strainer.

WHAT'S MISSING?

3 Years – 6 Years

WHAT YOU'LL NEED: various items from around your household.

Here's a fun game you can play with your child to work on a range of skills that will enhance your child's communication, from naming items to exercising short-term memory.

Begin by gathering a variety of items or images belonging to the same category. All items you choose should already be familiar to your child. For example, you could pick "clothing" (hat, socks, T-shirt) or "kitchen" (fork, plate, cup). Gather only a few items for an early learner. A more advanced learner may be able to work with more items. Have your child sit facing you and lay out the items between the two of you. Help your child name each item, and name its category, too, for extra language exposure. Explain to your child that they'll be covering their eyes so they can't see an item you'll be taking away from the group. Ask your child to then uncover their eyes and name which item is missing. This is the part of the game that exercises memory. If your child has difficulty recalling what's missing, try offering clues by naming each item for them. You can also reduce the number of items for the next round. To help more, you could give your child the choice between two items that may be missing, while naming both the one that's present and the one that's missing.

WHY THIS ACTIVITY WORKS

This activity works extensively on your child's receptive language, which is the ability to understand words, language, or gestures of others. Receptive language is typically the first type of language a child learns. For young children, this involves responding to the words and signals of others in concrete ways, such as understanding that when their mom stretches her arms out and says, "Hug me," she wants them to run over and give her a big hug. As a child matures, their receptive skills develop into the knowledge that when their mom picks up her keys, she's going to leave in the car and that a car is a large moving object with wheels, windows, and doors. Eventually, strong receptive skills will allow your child to comprehend the written words "Park car here."

TIP Using toys or items that your child enjoys, such as favorite foods or plush animals, can make this game even more engaging for your child.

MUSIC TO MY EARS

3 Years – 11 Years

WHAT YOU'LL NEED: music in any form.

All you'll need for this activity is music you can turn on and off with the touch of a button, or your own singing voice. Play or sing your child's favorite songs, then stop just before the end and allow your child to fill in the remaining one or two words. For example, if you're singing "Row, row, row your boat, gently down the stream," stop just before the word "stream" and allow your child to sing it by themselves. Singing with your child will bring improvements in verbalization and vocabulary. You'll be amazed at just how much language you'll hear from your child with this activity!

WHY THIS ACTIVITY WORKS

You may have heard that "a child who sings is a happy child." Even children who have significant struggles communicating with words often are miraculously fluid in their speech when singing a song. There's something about melody, harmonic rhythm, and the energy a song brings that attracts young listeners with autism and makes them want to sing along. This activity takes full advantage of this quality of music to elicit a variety of fluent communication and social skills from your child.

TIP If your child has a particularly strong interest in music, try using a singsongy voice to get their attention when giving directions or engaging in play. Music can increase cooperation in children with ASD. So joyfully sing away with your child every day!

WHAT'S THAT SMELL?

4 Years – 10 Years

WHAT YOU'LL NEED: things your child can smell.

For this activity, all you'll need are your child's nose and an array of strong scents. I chose the sense of smell for this activity because there's a strong link between our sense of smell and our emotions and memory. Even before birth, our olfactory receptors are fully formed, making our ability to smell the first of our senses to mature. You can use smell to elicit a variety of nonverbal communication responses in your learner.

Start by telling your child the main rule of the game: no talking allowed. Next, introduce your child to various ways they can express their opinion about what they smell by using nonverbal communication, such as gestures and facial expressions. They could give a thumbs-up, smile, or lick their lips for a pleasant smell, and offer a thumbs-down, frown, or stick out their tongue for a disgusting smell.

Give your learner one scent at time to smell. You can blindfold them for added excitement (if they're comfortable with that). Once they've taken a big whiff, see what they thought of it.

WHY THIS ACTIVITY WORKS

This activity focuses on nonverbal communication skills. Nonverbal communication can be a struggle for children with ASD, and this is evident when a young learner is unable to point, nod their head, or make eye contact to connect with the person they're talking to. All these nonverbal behaviors add meaning to what they're trying to communicate, and strengthening nonverbal communication is an important step in a child's development. This activity helps your child practice expressing themselves to develop these skills.

TIP For extra variety, you can also use this activity with the other four senses by tasting snack foods or condiments, touching various textures, looking at different kinds of artwork, and listening to an array of music genres.

CONVERSATION TOWER

5 Years – 11 Years

WHAT YOU'LL NEED: any kind of blocks. Optional: images and writing materials.

Start by sitting at a table or on the floor across from your child. Explain that you'll be using blocks to build a "conversation tower" together.

Begin by coming up with a topic to start your conversation. You may want to choose the first topic and then take turns choosing topics with your child each time you build a new tower. If your child has difficulty with conversations, make sure the topic is simple and fun, like "favorite foods." If they're a bit more

skilled in conversations, your topic can be slightly more complicated, like "summer vacations."

Next, explain that each block represents a question or comment in your conversation. Take turns making a statement, answering a question, or asking a question. Once a person contributes a question or comment to the conversation, they place one block on the tower. Challenge your child to keep the conversation going for as long as possible so you can create a tower that reaches the stars!

If your child can read, you can add extra support by giving a list of conversation starter topics or sample questions and comments to choose from. Some fun sample questions might be "What are the best dessert foods?" or "Describe your favorite cartoon character." If your child doesn't yet read, you can provide assistance by having visual images to give them ideas for responses. Put out pictures of animals, foods, family members, favorite TV characters, or fun event locations. Another variation is to write the actual questions and comments directly on the blocks as a guide.

WHY THIS ACTIVITY WORKS

The back-and-forth flow of a conversation is essential to your child's ability to connect and communicate with others. The ability to add to a topic by responding to what was meaningfully expressed by a conversation partner helps your child develop friendships and fit in. This skill often doesn't come naturally to children with ASD and therefore requires a lot of repetition. Using blocks as prompts for conversational exchanges is one way to work on taking turns in conversations.

TIP If this is a particularly challenging skill for your child , start with very simple exchanges for a short time and increase the complexity accordingly. Your starter conversation could go like this:

You: "What's your favorite color?"
Child: "Red."
Child: "What's your favorite color?"
You: "Purple."

INQUISITIVE QUESTIONER

5 Years – 11 Years

WHAT YOU'LL NEED: a set of blank note cards and something to write with.

Children are inquisitive, constantly curious about the world around them. Typically developing children begin to ask questions at about two-and-a-half years old to satisfy this curiosity. If your child needs assistance learning to ask questions, play this fun game to help them develop this valuable skill.

Create two decks of cards. For deck one, on each card write a question word or short phrase to start a question. For deck two, on each card write one noun word (person, place, or thing).

Example questions for deck one:

- "How do you . . . ?"
- "How . . . ?"
- "Where do you find . . . ?"
- "Where . . . ?"
- "What is the best way to . . . ?"
- "What . . . ?"
- "When will we . . . ?"
- "Who can you ask . . . ?"

Example noun words for deck two:

- dog
- banana
- school
- park
- postal carrier
- brother

To play the game, take turns picking up one card from each pile and asking a question using the words on the cards. For example, if your child chooses the card from deck one that says "How do you . . . ?" and the card from deck two says "banana," they would then ask the question "How do you peel a banana?" After answering your child's question, you then pick two cards and ask your question using the words on your cards. The game can go back and forth as long as the two of you are having fun.

WHY THIS ACTIVITY WORKS

For children with autism, the ability to ask questions may develop much later or not at all without encouragement. Playing this game with your child teaches them how to ask questions in order to develop their genuine interest in the acquisition of knowledge.

TIP If your child needs extra support with question-asking, you can write entire questions and allow your child to choose which questions they'd like to ask.

CHOCOLATE TIME

6 Years – 11 Years

WHAT YOU'LL NEED: milk or nondairy drink, chocolate or other flavoring, spoon. Optional: photos.

Giving precise instructions to someone to perform a task can be tricky, especially for a child with ASD who doesn't communicate easily. When giving an instruction, there's a lot to think about: the sequence of steps, the details of the description, and the clarity of articulation and tone of voice. Being able to effectively direct someone to complete a task is an important life skill that involves higher order thinking and cognitive development. This activity helps your child advance in their ability to sequence steps and give clear directions to another person in order to assist that person in completing a task.

Decide on a task your child will be motivated enough to instruct you to perform. Usually pouring a drink for a thirsty child or preparing a meal for a hungry child is a great place to start. Let's use "making chocolate milk" as an example. Begin by having your child observe you making chocolate milk a few times while you state each step aloud.

1. Get milk from fridge.

2. Get cup from cupboard.

3. Get chocolate powder from pantry.

4. Pour milk in cup.

5. Spoon chocolate powder into milk.

6. Mix milk and chocolate powder together.

Then on subsequent times your child wants a cold glass of chocolate milk, ask them to tell you step by step what to do while you perform each step. Complete each step your child directs you to do, even if they're incorrect. This is where this activity can get a little messy and very funny.

WHY THIS ACTIVITY WORKS
Learning a complicated skill like giving multistep instructions requires both repetition and positive reinforcement. Using a short and fun task like making chocolate milk will motivate your child to practice this skill with you over and over until they've mastered it.

TIP For a younger learner, accept simple directions of one or two words. You can also prepare a younger child for success with this task by having them sequence picture cards. To do this, before moving on to live practice, take photos of the six steps to make chocolate milk and rehearse by putting the cards in the correct order.

THE BARRIER GAME

7 Years – 11 Years

WHAT YOU'LL NEED: clay or two sets of blocks or crayons and paper. Optional: writing materials.

Once you've chosen the material, you and your child will sit back-to-back. One of you will be designated as the leader, who will call out directions, while the other will act as the student, who will follow the directions. The leader designs a simple structure or picture. Then they describe, step by step, to their student how to make it. The student can ask for clarification during this process. Once all the directions are given, you both turn around and compare your designs. Do they look alike? Where did the student make mistakes? How could the leader have been more descriptive? Discuss the details and giggle over the differences, then switch roles. It's fun to keep track of how many of the designs match.

WHY THIS ACTIVITY WORKS

Children with autism who have strong verbal skills may still have some challenges with language and communication. They often have difficulty producing and comprehending words that describe something. Attending to the fine details involved in communication can be a daunting task that takes a lot of practice to master. This activity is a fun way to work on these skills with older and more advanced learners.

TIP If needed, you can start by sitting face-to-face so you can assist your child in understanding and giving directions. Then move on to trying the game back-to-back when your child is ready. You may also want to give your child written prompts to assist them with ideas for how to clearly explain their design.

CHAPTER FOUR

LET'S DO SOMETHING TOGETHER!

Many clinical experts believe children with autism have difficulty developing a "theory of mind," which includes the capacity to recognize that others hold an internal mental state different from their own. As a result, they may not be able to comprehend that other people have personal experiences of knowledge, emotions, and expectations. One example of the absence of strong "theory of mind" skills would be a child who isn't able to predict the feelings of a person who has just experienced a disappointing event. When shown a video of a child who just watched their ice cream cone fall to the floor, a child with ASD may not be able to predict that the child in the video will likely be feeling sad as a result.

Doing something together requires that we share our attention with others and focus on the same thing at the same time. This is called *joint attention*—the ability to share focus on an object or experience with another person. The end goal of joint attention is the ability to share in the enjoyment of an event with someone else. Joint attention is how we connect with other people. Knowing that someone else delights in our presence gives us a feeling of warmth and pleasure. Often, one of the first and most noticeable indicators that a young child has autism is their inability to display joint attention skills such as responding to their name when called, pointing to an object, imitating others' facial expressions, and seeking comfort in a parent when upset.

The inability to recognize other people's point of view or predict the emotional state of others is likely a contributor to the difficulty children with autism have in making friends and participating in joint activities, which involve two or more people engaging in a shared goal. Once your child learns to share the focus of their attention with another person and understands the causes of different emotional states, they'll be better equipped to participate in rewarding relationships.

The activities in this chapter assist you in teaching your child to engage in shared emotional experiences, predict how their words and actions will affect other people's feelings, and understand there are differences in each person's point of view. As you participate in the following activities, you'll see your child's joint attention skills strengthen and observe your child increase their emotional connections with those around them.

ONE LITTLE FINGER

1 Year – 3 Years

WHAT YOU'LL NEED: "One Little Finger" song. (You can easily find it online.)

One of the earliest indicators that a child may have autism is their inability to point. Typically, children begin to point when they're about 15 months old. This is one of their first forms of communication. They usually begin with *imperative pointing*—pointing at something because they want it and want you to get it for them. Then they move on to *declarative pointing*—showing something to you or sharing in the experience with you. Although pointing is a quick gesture, there's a complex cognitive process involved. This step-by-step activity will help teach your child this valuable skill.

MODELING: It's always a good idea to begin by demonstrating a skill before you require your child to do it. A good place to start is to model what pointing looks like while you sing the song "One Little Finger" together. (You can find online videos to learn this song.)

HAND-OVER-HAND HELP: Form your child's hand into a point and hold this pointing position if necessary while you sing "One Little Finger."

PRACTICE: Follow "One Little Finger" directions of pointing your finger up and down, then pointing to a specified body part.

GENERALIZE: Practice this skill during your child's daily life. Have your child point to the snack they prefer when you offer them two options. Or help your child point to items in a book you read together. Pop bubbles with a pointed finger or point to an airplane in the sky they're excited to see and share with you.

WHY THIS ACTIVITY WORKS
This is a very effective teaching activity because it incorporates multiple evidence-based practices for teaching children with autism, including modeling, prompting, and positive reinforcement.

TIP "Where is Thumbkin?" is another great song to sing and practice finger pointing with your child. No child is ever too young or old to learn this skill.

ROUGH-AND-TUMBLE

2 Years – 8 Years

WHAT YOU'LL NEED: nothing needed for this activity. Optional: a towel or blanket.

To do rough-and-tumble with your child, find an activity you know your child will enjoy. You can pull your child on a blanket across the floor, twirl them around in circles in the yard, or chase them from room to room, giving a strong tickle once they're captured. Do as much or as little as you have the energy for and they enjoy.

Here's a bonus opportunity: Incorporate opportunities for your child to ask for more. This usually involves stopping the activity at the climax. For example, give your child a few rounds of chase that ends in a tickle when they're captured, then the next time stop right before the tickle with your hands up, fingers wiggling. Your child will most likely be anticipating the tickle and therefore look right in your eyes or give you a gleaming smile. This is excellent communication. When you feel your child has connected with you to ask for more or has made a verbal request, lay those tickles on them!

WHY THIS ACTIVITY WORKS
Physical play has lots of benefits for children, especially those with autism. Physical play with your child uplifts mood, fulfills sensory needs, strengthens muscles, improves coordination, enhances concentration, and aids in sleep—just to name a few. Physical play is also a very effective way to motivate your child to engage with you in a joint activity that will leave them wanting more.

TIP This is also a great opportunity to work on your child responding to their name or gaining your attention by calling for you, tapping your shoulder, or taking your hand. During this play, they'll be highly inspired to use their verbal and nonverbal skills to engage you in more play. Once they master this skill with you, have someone you trust take your place so your child can generalize the shared engagement skills and build a strong connection with others.

EMOTIONS BOOK

3 Years – 7 Years

WHAT YOU'LL NEED: a camera, printer, and stapler.

Just like everyone else, children with ASD experience a wide range of emotions. Often, though, they find it difficult to label their emotions and to identify other people's emotions. This can make it seem like they have less concern or empathy for others. It also makes them less equipped with the know-how to share an emotion with a family member or friend, and it can be harder to comfort them. Making an emotions book with your child is a great way to practice identifying emotions.

MAKING AN EMOTIONS BOOK

1. Use a camera to capture your child displaying various emotions. (You can also use pictures of other family members.)

2. Print the images.

3. Staple the pictures together into a small book.

USING YOUR EMOTIONS BOOK

1. Help your child become familiar with and identify the emotions in the pictures.

2. Discuss what scenarios and events make people feel each emotion.

3. Use your child's emotions book to help them explain their feelings as they're happening.

Some common beginner-level emotions to consider including in your book:

- Happy
- Sad
- Excited
- Surprised
- Angry
- Overwhelmed
- Frustrated
- Scared

WHY THIS ACTIVITY WORKS

Because your child is going to love flipping through the pages of the emotions book to see their own dramatic expressions, they'll be highly engaged in this activity.

TIP Make the book compact and carry it with you, especially when you know you'll encounter a situation that triggers a strong emotion for your child. Help them use the experience to label how they're feeling at the time.

SEARCHLIGHT

3 Years – 8 Years

WHAT YOU'LL NEED: a small flashlight or laser pointer and some items to hide.

This activity develops joint attention skills (sharing focus). There are three key elements for achieving joint attention: your child, you, and an object/occurrence.

Begin by hiding the items in various locations around a room or your home. Next, hand your child the flashlight and explain they'll be using it to search for each item you name. Give them the name of the first item, and then go on the hunt with them to find it. Once they find the item, make sure your child shines the light on it so you know the item has their attention. Then offer praise by making an excited sound or exclamation to get your child to glance up at you, shifting their focus from the found item over to you. Now, have your child retrieve the found item and see if you can get them to comment on their shared experience with you.

For children with less verbal language, model saying the name of the item in a happy voice and try to get them to copy you. For children with more verbal language, encourage them to say a full sentence, such as "I found the Spider-Man book!" Continue this sequence until they find all items. Now, pat yourself on the back because once you're successful getting your child to play the searchlight game, you're on your way to developing your child's joint attention. This valuable skill will lead them to form strong relationships with many important people in their life!

WHY THIS ACTIVITY WORKS
One of the main reasons this activity is so effective is that it uses the evidence-based practice of naturalistic teaching—*a child is learning while practicing the new skill in the actual environment where the skill will later be used, rather than in a structured environment not related to the skill being taught. In addition, you're using positive reinforcement to strengthen their joint attention skills.*

TIP Don't get discouraged if this is a challenging task for your child. Joint attention is a complex skill to develop. Continue to practice this while giving your child a lot of praise and recognition for a job well done. For advanced learners, make the items harder to find and include clues to tell them if they're "hot" or "cold" while searching.

FUNNY FEATURES

5 Years – 11 Years

WHAT YOU'LL NEED: several strips of paper and something to write with. Optional: photos or drawings.

This activity is geared toward advanced learners who have some pretend play skills. On half the strips of paper, write names of family members, friends, teachers, and animals. On the rest, write various features, such as: can breathe under water, has a billion dollars in the bank, has wings, or has green reptile skin. Keep the names and features groups separate and place them in two bowls or in two piles on the floor. Have your child pick one word from each group.

Now you're ready to ask questions. For example, if your child chose the words "dog" and "has wings," you could ask, "What would happen if your dog had wings?" Help your child think of ideas for what this would be like. Allow for silly responses as long as they make sense in the context. A possible response may be, "If my dog had wings, he would fly over our doggie gate and eat the bacon from the kitchen counter." Or "If my dog had wings, he would be best friends with our pet parrot." This is a fun activity to use during a playdate. Allow your child and friend to ask each other questions and laugh at their imaginative ideas.

WHY THIS ACTIVITY WORKS

The abstract mind is imaginative, inquisitive, and interested in finding out the deeper meaning of a concept—as opposed to the concrete mind, which tends to focus on facts and literal meanings in the physical world. It's important for children to have a healthy balance of abstract and concrete thinking so they can generalize learning from one context to the other. This activity nurtures your child's abstract intelligence, unlocking their creativity and helping them see things from new angles.

TIP With a younger child, you may want to use pictures rather than words. For example, one picture could be of very large crocodile teeth and another picture could be of your child's grandma. The child would then use the pictures to create the sentence "If my grandma had crocodile teeth, she could eat a mountain of popcorn."

THINK VS. SAY

5 Years – 11 Years

WHAT YOU'LL NEED: paper and something to write with.

This three-step activity helps your child develop social communication skills.

STEP 1: Differentiate between the concepts of "think" and "say" so your child understands what each word means. Explain to your child, "*Think* means talking to yourself in your head, and only you can hear your thoughts. *Say* means things that you talk out of your mouth, and others can hear."

STEP 2: Create two visual aids: One will be an image of a "thought bubble," and the other a "speech bubble" like in a comic book. Give your child a sample comment and see if they can tell you which bubble it should be in. For example, "Jill's singing is ugly and hurts my ears." Ask, "Should this comment stay in your head or is it okay say it out loud in front of Jill?"

STEP 3: Talk to your child about why it's important to filter their thoughts. "How would Jill feel if you told her out loud that her singing is ugly and hurts your ears?"

WHY THIS ACTIVITY WORKS
When a child develops "theory of mind," a higher order social-cognitive skill, they understand that others' perceptions, thoughts, and feelings or beliefs may be different from their own. This is an important kind of thinking to develop, and it will help your child navigate their social sphere more smoothly. This activity helps your child become a thoughtful social communicator. Your child will learn to recognize what should stay only as a thought in their head versus what's acceptable to say out loud.

TIP A fun way to practice this valuable skill with a younger child is to use the "thought bubble" and "speech bubble" visuals while you read books with pictures. Have your child decipher what the characters may be saying or thinking in the pictures.

EMOTION CHARADES

6 Years – 10 Years

WHAT YOU'LL NEED: strips of paper, something to write with, and a bowl.

This family activity builds on the skills learned in the creation of the earlier "Emotions Book" activity. Once your child has a verbal repertoire of emotions, you can advance their knowledge and understanding of emotions with this game.

You'll first prepare for this game by writing several emotion labels on individual strips of paper. Then fold the strips over so the words are hidden and place them in a bowl.

HOW TO PLAY EMOTION CHARADES

1. The first player picks an emotion label from the bowl.

2. The player acts out the emotion they've chosen using only actions, not words. (You'll want to pick first to model this for your child.)

3. The audience guesses the emotion being displayed, yelling out possible answers.

4. The audience member who yells out the correct answer first wins the round!

WHY THIS ACTIVITY WORKS

Role play is an evidence-based practice and effective method of teaching a child with ASD to understand complex situations. You're bound to see your child make a lot of progress quickly during this fun game.

TIP To make this game more complicated, the presenter can act out a scenario along with displaying emotions. The audience then needs to guess both the emotion and the cause of the emotion. For example, if the emotion is "excited," the scenario acted out could be "excited because you scored the winning soccer goal for your team."

DOUBLE DARE

6 Years – 11 Years

WHAT YOU'LL NEED: nothing needed for this activity. Optional: index cards and something to write with.

You and your child will take turns daring each other to perform various actions. For example, say to your child, "I bet you can't tap your head and rub your tummy at the same time." Then laugh and praise each other for your efforts. For a beginner learner, you can treat this as a game of imitation, starting with simple one-step directions and increasing the complexity as your child gets better at it. For more advanced learners, challenge each other with directions of three to five steps that become increasingly wacky as the game progresses.

Zany example actions:

- Pretend to be a pair of scissors.
- Draw your name with your foot.
- Hide your head in your shirt and count by twos.

WHY THIS ACTIVITY WORKS
Playing Double Dare with your child is an excellent way to share in a joint experience. This game promotes eye contact, imitation, communication, direction giving and following, and self-esteem.

TIP You can always write the steps on index cards. This will help your child remember them and make the game more fluid. If your child struggles with multistep instructions, use directions you know they have experience with.

SAME AND DIFFERENT

6 Years – 11 Years

WHAT YOU'LL NEED: paper and something to write with.

For this activity, you assist your child in creating a comparison between themselves and the closest people in their lives. Take a sheet of paper and draw a line down the middle. Write your child's name at the top on one side and the name of the person they're comparing themselves to on the other side. Think of ways that both individuals are similar. You can begin with physical features and move on to areas of their lives, such as where they live and things they enjoy. Write these items together and discuss the likenesses.

WHY THIS ACTIVITY WORKS

Perspective-taking is a higher order cognitive skill. This skill is directly linked with our ability to empathize with someone else. To help our children with autism develop empathy it's essential that we teach them to see the similarities they have with others. This is also true for nurturing in your child a sense of care for their siblings or peers. The more your child sees they have in common with others, the better able they are to relate to them and have compassion.

TIP For a more experienced learner, you can also make comparisons that include differences. If your child likes chocolate desserts and you like fruity desserts, you can add this to your lists. You can ask questions such as, "Would you enjoy going out for chocolate ice cream?" and "Would Mommy want to go get chocolate ice cream?" to gauge your child's understanding of others' points of view. For children less experienced with this skill, you can begin by having your child exchange comments with others about their favorite things in various subject areas.

CONFIDENCE CUBE

8 Years – 11 Years

WHAT YOU'LL NEED: an empty tissue box or other lightweight cube-shaped item you can toss around, blank paper, and glue or tape.

For this game, the cube will act as your dice. Glue white paper to each side of the cube. Then, write sentence beginnings on each side of your dice. Once the game begins, you and your child will fill in the missing part of the sentence, as you take turns rolling the dice. For example, one sentence could be "I feel proud of myself when I . . . " All the responses will focus on emphasizing your child's positive characteristics and talents. Using prompts this way will help your child cognitively retrieve positive responses about themselves when faced with challenges in everyday life. Play this game every so often to keep these positive affirmations in the forefront of your mind and your child's mind.

EXAMPLE SENTENCES TO USE:

- I'm really good at . . .
- I feel happy when . . .
- I'm most creative when I . . .
- It's very cool that I can . . .
- People who know me well really like that I . . .

WHY THIS ACTIVITY WORKS

This activity teaches children what's great about themselves and increases their overall self-esteem. If your child plays often enough, they'll always have a self-compliment on the tip of their tongue when they need a pick-me-up.

TIP For a twist on this activity, create a compliment cube with the names of your child's closest family and friends. Take turns rolling the dice and complimenting the person who comes up. For example, for the name "Mom," your child will say something like "Mom is fun to play games with."

CHAPTER FIVE

LET'S PLAY!

Playing offers crucial learning opportunities for children to strengthen a wide variety of skills they'll need later in life. Because children with autism typically lack naturally developing play skills, they don't get the chance to practice social skills and expand their communication skills through play. They also miss out on engaging in the fun and imaginative playtime other children enjoy.

Play actions are building blocks to other skills. Children learn to request desired items when they ask for their favorite toy character during play. Children can expand their labeling skills (pointing out things they notice in the environment) when they're playing with a toy airplane and suddenly exclaim, "The plane is flying so high." Children practice conversation, compromise, and negotiation during imaginative play as a group and act out and discuss a wide range of pretend scenarios. They also rehearse future life skills during make-believe time, like playing house or pretending to feed the dog, fix the car, or cook dinner.

Helping your child develop robust and varied play skills will benefit them greatly, now and in the future. Your child will build on these skills to strengthen communication and socialization with others. This chapter provides fun activities you can use to nurture your child's abilities in a variety of play skills, each building on the next. The play skills taught in these activities include exploratory play, imaginative play, solitary or independent play, parallel play, symbolic or pretend play, and cooperative play, which includes sharing and turn-taking.

I CAN PLAY BY MYSELF

1 Year – 5 Years

WHAT YOU'LL NEED: some simple activities your child will be interested in exploring.

For this activity, toys that light up, make noise, and have various textures, shapes, and colors have a good chance of capturing your child's attention. Preferably these activities will be close-ended, which means they'll have a clear start and finish point. (You can choose toys that can be played with in one step—such as moving a train down a track—or several steps, such as completing a shape sorter.) It's a good idea to put these toys away until you introduce them one at a time to your child.

First, you'll want to demonstrate for your child how to play with the chosen toy. Ooh and aah over it with lots of expression so you're more likely to pique your child's curiosity. Next, offer the toy to your child. Watch them to see if they imitate the actions you've displayed. Give it a little time, and if they don't imitate your actions, take your child's hand and guide them to do the action correctly. Remember to praise your child for a job well done. Soon you'll be able to step aside and watch your child enjoy a wide variety of toys during independent playtime.

IDEAS FOR TOYS TO START WITH:

- Toddler books with a few pages
- Simple puzzles with knobs for easier handling
- Dressing a doll
- Stringing chunking beads
- A jar to drop pennies in

WHY THIS ACTIVITY WORKS

Solitary play, *also called independent play, is the first level of play socialization and involves play in which a child manipulates a toy, as it's intended for, by themselves. This activity helps your child develop solitary play skills through modeling, prompting, and positive reinforcement.*

TIP Often when a child plays alone, automatic reinforcement behaviors may interfere with play—for example, eye gazing with the wheels of a car toy or repeating the lines of a video watched earlier while completing a puzzle. When this occurs, it's best to interrupt the behavior and redirect your child to use actions or speech appropriate for the toy in front of them.

WE'RE FOLLOWING THE LEADER

1 Year – 5 Years

WHAT YOU'LL NEED: various items and activities from around the house and small treats or toys for rewards.

Imitation is the act of copying someone else's behavior. Children learn and make connections with others by imitating behaviors. The best way to increase your child's imitation skills is through games and play.

HERE ARE THE STEPS TO TEACH IMITATION, WHILE PLAYING THE GAME "FOLLOW THE LEADER":

1. Demonstrate the play action you would like your child to perform. Examples include tapping a drum, crashing toy cars, ringing a bell, rolling dough, tossing a ball, or drawing a circle, square, or happy face.

2. Give your child the instruction "Copy me," "Your turn," or "Do this."

3. Help your child so they can successfully copy the play action you demonstrated.

4. Immediately give your child a preferred food, praise, or toy.

5. Gradually fade out the amount of assistance you give your child to copy your play action so they'll become more independent with this skill and eventually be able to do it independently.

6. Encourage all family members to play this game with your child.

WHY THIS ACTIVITY WORKS
For a child with ASD, imitation can be difficult, and learning skills such as play, social interaction, language, and daily living activities can be affected. Using the steps in this activity, your child will develop the skill of copying through modeling, prompting, and positive reinforcement.

THE MAGIC BOX

1 Year – 7 Years

WHAT YOU'LL NEED: various small items from around the home.

For this activity, things like a toilet tissue roll, paper plate, fork, plastic container, pen, paper, flower, rock, and banana are perfect. Place all the items in a box you'll call the "magic box." Explain to your child that you'll call out the name of a toy, and they need to find something in the box that will magically become that toy. For example, if you say "car," your child may pick out the toilet tissue roll or a pen and say "vroom" while they move it back and forth on the floor. It's a good idea to demonstrate for your child how to play the game first.

Start with only two or three items for your child to choose from. Then, slowly add more items as they show success with symbolic play with a few toys. With more advanced learners, you can elaborate on your play scenarios or ask your child to come up with their own ideas for how to use the items in the magic box. There's an infinite number of ideas to take your child's imagination and yours outside the box!

WHY THIS ACTIVITY WORKS

When a child engages in symbolic play, they're displaying their ability to think creatively by turning an ordinary object into a functional toy. This form of play is a crucial part of a child's intellectual development as it's the link between functional pretend play and imaginary play. This activity helps younger children grow their cognitive flexibility and expand their repertoire of play skills.

THE JOY OF READING

1 Year – 11 Years

WHAT YOU'LL NEED: children's books.

Reading is an enjoyable activity that falls under the category of independent play. Some children with autism don't have a wide variety of fun things to do when given time to play by themselves at home. Here are 10 tips for making reading your child's new favorite pastime!

- Have your child choose the book to read. If they tend to always pick the same book, do a book rotation. Make sure particular books are available only one time each day, week, or month.
- Use different funny voices for each character in the story, and when they're ready to read, have your child be one character and you be the others.
- Make connections between the characters or events in the story and your child's real life.
- Pick a page in the book to act out, using simple props and dress-up costumes.
- Create an enjoyable reading area in your home with plenty of sensory-friendly and super cuddly pillows, blankets, and stuffed toys.
- Let your child who loves art know they'll get to draw a picture about what happened in the book after it's complete. You could also draw alternative endings to the book.
- Ask your child questions during the book. For example, have your child practice labeling, letter or word recognition, and emotions.
- Take advantage of story time at your local library, often available for free. This is also a great opportunity to practice social skills.
- Find nonfiction and out-of-the-ordinary reading material on topics your child may find interesting, such as cookbooks, outer space, comic books, or magazines about race cars or animal species.
- Combine your book reading time with reinforcement. Reward your child with whatever is reinforcing for them while you read to them, whether it's small pieces of a preferred snack, high fives, tickles, or back scratches. They'll soon connect reading with receiving their favorite things and learn to love the special reading time you spend together.

WHY THIS ACTIVITY WORKS

Reading books to children every day is one of the greatest gifts you can give them. Reading improves language, empathy, and imagination and can impart the love of reading for a lifetime. For some children with autism, limited concentration may make it difficult to sit through a lengthy book. This can impede their interest in reading overall. This activity will give you some ideas for how to make reading books to children with ASD— who may need extra support—lively and entertaining.

FEEDING THE BEAR

3 Years – 7 Years

WHAT YOU'LL NEED: a plush bear or similar toy or doll and small treats for reward. Optional: index cards and something to write with.

Here's a fun way you can support a child who already has the ability to imitate simple actions in gaining the skills to use toys in functional pretend play. (See We're Following the Leader on page 49 for details on how to teach your child to imitate simple actions.) In this activity, instead of teaching an entire play sequence all at once, which **may be over-whelming** to your child, you'll be breaking down a play skill into multiple steps, teaching one at a time.

HOW TO PERFORM "FEEDING THE BEAR"

1. Hold the bear and imagine all the various actions that can be taught around this toy. For example, play actions could be to feed it, rock it, make it talk, and put it to bed.

2. Choose the easiest action first and show your child how to complete the action.

3. Hand the bear to your child and provide the necessary help they need to do the same actions.

4. Remember to provide a reinforcement reward when your child imitates your play actions. This will motivate your child to continue to practice these play sequences.

5. Slowly increase the complexity of the sequence of steps and fade your help (prompts). You'll quickly see the positive impact this has on your child's confidence during pretend play.

WHY THIS ACTIVITY WORKS

Functional pretend play—*play that involves using lifelike toys to demonstrate lifelike behaviors—is one of the earlier types of play a child performs. An example is playing with a kid-size kitchen toy set to cook plastic eggs in a toy pan and serve them to a friend. Kids with autism often lack the imitative behaviors and social communication skills needed for this type of play. Instead of playing appropriately, they may manipulate toys in a repetitive manner and be unresponsive to peers seeking to engage them in play. This activity will help your child build the skills necessary for functional pretend play.*

TIP It can also help to prepare in advance for the guided play by labeling individual index cards with steps 1, 2, and 3 for a variety of play actions and preparing edible reinforcement, like a small piece of your child's favorite snack.

IMAGINE THAT

3 Years – 9 Years

WHAT YOU'LL NEED: a homemade video recording.

For children with autism, the advanced form of play called *imaginative play* could be limited or nonexistent without external support. The ability to make believe they're Superman flying through the sky when they have no cape and can't actually fly may be out of the realm of possibility for a child with ASD.

A great way to introduce a child to imaginative play is by using video modeling, where a child observes a videotaped model engaging in a target play behavior. The actions observed are then practiced with a caregiver. Video modeling can be very effective for children with autism, and I'm sure you can imagine why. What child doesn't love watching videos? You can make the videos using yourself or your child's sibling in the starring role or by filming your child self-modeling the target behavior. Don't forget that your child may need assistance to display the specific play skill that you are teaching.

1. Record a short video (30 seconds) of you, your child, or your child's sibling acting out an imaginary play scene with toy figurines.

2. The video will depict a short sequence of interactions between two play characters. For example, your dog figurine could bark at the postal carrier, then see a cat, and then jump over a pillow while chasing the cat across the floor. The cat could then jump into a small box, close the lid, and begin meowing loudly.

3. Have your child watch the video several times before attempting to imitate what they see in the video.

4. Help your child copy what they've seen in the video until they don't need the video to act out the imaginary play sequence.

5. The final goal would be for your child to modify the play sequence by adding their own actions to the storyline.

WHY THIS ACTIVITY WORKS

Play is a safe place for kids to experiment with language, try out a variety of social interactions, and explore feelings. While growing intellectually from play, children are better equipped to navigate the world around them.

BEAUTIFUL FRIENDSHIPS

3 Years – 11 Years

WHAT YOU'LL NEED: some favorite toys. Optional: a favorite drink and snack.

Hosting a playdate can nurture a connection between your child and a peer and will help your child be better equipped to build bonds and make lasting friendships. Facilitating a successful playdate takes practice and lots of planning.

1. Before you begin to plan for a playdate, make sure to expose your child to an array of toys and activities so they will have some playtime experience.

2. Gather your child's preferred toys and have them ready to incorporate into the playdate.

3. Select a peer for the playdate. If you have options, pick the child who is the most patient, polite, and willing to go along with adults' directions.

4. Observe the playdate and jump in with assistance as needed. Your child may need help finding the language necessary to communicate their desires to the friend or following along with the desires of the new playmate.

For beginner learners, you may start by working on *parallel play*—the children play with similar toys, independent of one another while tolerating being near each other. Once this skill is mastered, you can move on to *associative play*—the children play with the same toys with the only interaction being to give, take, and share play materials. Act as the facilitator to prompt each child to exchange toys.

For advanced learners, you can work on cooperative and imaginative play skills, such as initiating play, joining play, expressing thoughts, role playing, and following a peer's rules and ideas. It can help to narrate for your child what's going on during the play. Ask the peer to talk directly to your child, then prompt your child to respond if they don't do it independently.

WHY THIS ACTIVITY WORKS
Peer-mediated instruction takes place when a typically developing friend or sibling models a behavior to help a child with ASD learn the new skill. It's an evidence-based practice for teaching children with autism and a very effective method of teaching new play skills.

TIP Keep the first few playdates short so you can end them on a good note. Make an effort not to be overly intrusive by allowing your child the opportunity to try to engage by themselves. Constantly reinforce the newfound friendship with lots of praise and special treats.

MY TURN, YOUR TURN

4 Years – 11 Years

WHAT YOU'LL NEED: a board game for young kids, index cards, colored markers, and a small favorite treat.

Taking turns is a way of organizing our engagement with others, with the most common example being the back-and-forth social reciprocity of a conversation. Early in life, children practice this life skill through toy and game play. In this activity, you'll learn how to use a simple board game to teach your child how to take turns.

I'll use the classic children's game "Candy Land" as an example, but see the tip for other great games. There are a few things you can do to adapt your game to younger children to help them understand the concept of taking turns, while minimizing frustration.

Visual aid: Create a visual support that will help cue your child when it's their turn. On one side of an index card, write in red "Your Turn," then on the other side write in green "My Turn." Flip this card during play to indicate whose turn it is.

Manipulate materials: In the game of "Candy Land," take out the character cards from the start of the path and single-color cards, so you're using only character cards from the end of the path and the double-color cards. This will make the game more enjoyable for an early learner, allowing your child to reach the end of the path quickly and successfully.

Easing the wait time: For children who have difficulty waiting for their turn, count down slowly from 10 until it's their turn, or use a quick cell phone timer, and let your child watch it to ease their anxiety while they wait.

Enticing reinforcement: Instead of the only end goal being "to win the game," add an extra-special prize to the end of the path, such as a piece of your child's favorite treat. This will surely motivate them to want to take turns like a pro!

WHY THIS ACTIVITY WORKS
This activity will likely be very successful in teaching your child to take turns during a game because it includes several evidence-based practices for teaching children with autism, including visual supports and positive reinforcement.

TIP Other good board game options:

- Barnyard Bingo
- Don't Break the Ice
- Pop-Up Pirate
- Zingo!
- Chutes and Ladders
- Hoot Owl Hoot!

SHARE THE PEAR

4 Years – 11 Years

WHAT YOU'LL NEED: any item to hold and pass and a timer.

Sharing shows caring, and it's fun! Sharing is a valuable play skill. Children who share well with their peers will inevitably learn to cooperate and make more friends.

This activity involves playing a game called Share the Pear, which is essentially a spin on "Hot Potato." This can be played with any item as long as it's not highly preferred by your child. You want your child to be willing to share it.

Set the timer based on how long you think your child can sustain their attention, and add time as they improve. You, your child, and anyone else available to play will simply pass the "pear" among the players until the timer goes off. The person who's left holding the "pear" loses and is out of the game. During the game, make sure to encourage your child to be a "good sharer," which they'll want to do so they won't be stuck with the "pear" when the music stops.

WHY THIS ACTIVITY WORKS
Differential reinforcement is an evidence-based practice for teaching children with autism. It means that reinforced behaviors will increase while nonreinforced behaviors will decrease. In this game, when your child shares, they're reinforced (stay in the game); when they don't share and are caught with the pear, they're not reinforced (out of the round).

TIP Another, more challenging spin on this game is to wrap a shareable surprise in many layers of wrapping paper. Pass the surprise around, and when the timer goes off, the player left holding it unwraps a layer. Keep playing until the surprise is completely revealed. The winner, left holding the surprise, must share it among all players. Choose a prize that's easily shared, such as clay, markers and paper, or a small package of cookies. Your child will likely to want to keep holding on to the surprise without passing it so they can open it. Make the rule that if you count to five and the player hasn't passed it, they are out.

THE SPECIAL HAT

4 Years – 11 Years

WHAT YOU'LL NEED: a hat.

Cooperative play is the most advanced form of play a child can engage in. It involves two or more children using the same toys to work together for a common goal. This activity assists children who may appear bossy or inflexible when they play, when in reality, they just need support to let go of their anxiety surrounding novel cooperative play opportunities.

Before your child begins to play with you, a sibling, or a friend, designate a leader who wears a special hat during cooperative play. The person wearing the hat chooses what they'll play and the rules of playing while the others follow along. Make sure to trade off being the leader and give all participants an equal amount of time wearing the special hat.

WHY THIS ACTIVITY WORKS

Often, children with ASD find it easier to display a specific behavior when given a rule or set of rules explaining what's expected. In this activity, you're giving your child the rule "whoever wears the hat is the leader and is in charge of play while all others not wearing the hat must follow along." Once your child has played often enough using this rule, they'll likely become accustomed to taking turns being the leader during play and should no longer need the aid of the hat.

CHAPTER SIX

LET'S GET SOCIAL!

Almost everything we do is enhanced when we share it with others. Our ability to share special moments with one another is part of what makes our lives enjoyable and meaningful. Many children with ASD find it difficult to interact with the people in their family, at school, and in their community. This creates social challenges that can prevent them from participating in many significant experiences, and it can close access to important opportunities. Once a child with autism has been taught the necessary skills to succeed in a social interaction, they feel tremendous joy and satisfaction from engaging in shared experiences with others.

The foundational social skills that many children with ASD find most difficult include eye contact, joint (shared) attention, and imitation. These basic skills are vital for every child to learn because they pave the way for so many other skills to be developed as the child matures. Typically developing children naturally learn to look at faces and make eye contact. Recognizing facial expressions gives a child one more way to make sense of the world around them. *Joint attention*—the ability to share focus on an object or experience with another person—is also essential in developing close social relationships with others because it connects people to each other and creates social bonds. Imitation skills involve the ability to accurately copy someone's behavior. This is another core area that can be challenging for children diagnosed with autism. The importance of children using imitation to learn cannot be over-stated. Almost every other skill a child learns comes from imitating those around them. The wide variety of skills a child will learn using their ability to imitate others ranges from using a spoon to asking a new friend to play.

Gaining attention from others, giving compliments, being appropriately assertive, taking turns, and apologizing are advanced social skills that are just as important to a child's social development. In my clinical experience, I've met many children who lack the ability to appropriately gain attention from others. This leads them to seek attention through the display of negative behaviors, and it often leaves the child feeling lonely and isolated because their appropriate attempts to connect socially go unnoticed by others. All these skills can be successfully taught and are often the most enjoyable for children to learn. By using the simple activities in this book, you and your child will be on your way to more successful communication and social engagement.

MAKING CHOICES

2 Years – 5 Years

WHAT YOU'LL NEED: any available food and items from around the home.

This activity is a way to help a child who has limited communication and language skills display the social skill of responding to a question. Often, children with ASD who have speech delays or disorders know what you are asking them and what they want to say, but they're unable to get the words out. This frustrating situation can lead to problem behaviors. This choice-making activity outlines an easy method to help your child actively participate in responding to you and making their decisions and preferences known.

You'll first need to teach your child the steps to making a choice.

1. **PICK THE OPTIONS:** Whenever possible, use the actual items when presenting your child with a choice. For example, if you would like your child to tell you which dessert they want after dinner, present two possibilities—say, a dish of ice cream or cookies.

2. **OFFER THE OPTIONS:** When you know your child is motivated, put the desserts out on the table or hold them where your child can see them and ask, "Which dessert would you like?" You will know your child is motivated and has a strong desire for the item if they are closely following the movement of the item with their eyes or reaching out to grab the item.

3. **WAIT FOR A RESPONSE:** If they do not point to, reach for, or look at an option, ask the question again and guide their hand forward.

4. **GIVE THE SELECTED OPTION IMMEDIATELY:** If your child appears satisfied with their choice, praise them for making the choice and prompt them to say the name of the item. If the item is instead refused, remove it. Never force a child to take what they choose if they don't want it. Repeat the above steps removing the option they refused or moving it further away from them to make it less likely they will choose it.

You can use the Making Choices activity for questions that are simple or complex. There are endless opportunities to present your child with choices throughout the day.

- Picking out preferred options for food to eat, clothing to wear, outing locations (use images of locations)
- Terminating an activity ("stop" or "keep playing" images)
- Telling others how they're feeling (facial expression images)
- Asking what they did at school that day (use images to represent activities)

Using visuals (either a picture or the actual item) to give children with autism choices allows them to have a way of communicating functionally, feel a sense of control, and gain personal independence in their daily lives.

POLITE ALL DAY LONG, WITH A GOOD MANNERS SONG

2 Years – 9 Years

WHAT YOU'LL NEED: nothing needed for this activity.

In this activity, you'll be playing with language to help your child learn what it looks and sounds like to be polite. Often, politeness does not come instinctively to individuals with autism. If your child is struggling to remember their manners, you can take a few steps to help them master the social skills of polite behavior. First, it's a good idea to share why politeness is so important. Express to your child how being polite can make others feel valued, appreciated, and respected. Second, you can use this activity to have fun while helping your child remember the rules of politeness.

SING THE FOLLOWING SIMPLE RHYMING LINES WITH YOUR CHILD (MAKE UP ANY TUNE!):

Good manners are like flowers, they have magic powers.

I cover my mouth when I cough and sneeze, so my germs don't blow in the breeze.

When you bump into a friend who was in your way, just say "I'm sorry" and it's all okay.

With my friends I always share, and they know how much I care.

"Please" and "thank you" are things I say when I want a toy or to eat or play.

Waiting my turn in line at school makes me feel really cool.

Eye contact shows that I care about what my friends have to share.

When I'm all done, cleaning up is fun.

WHY THIS ACTIVITY WORKS
Language play is a great way to help your child acquire new vocabulary, practice grammar skills, and learn the rules of politeness in a fun and silly way. Rhyming words are catchy and easily remembered, helping your child memorize and display good manners.

TIP If your child has advanced communication skills, the two of you can make up rhymes together to remember specific politeness rules within your household.

TOPIC TALK

3 Years – 7 Years

WHAT YOU'LL NEED: nothing needed for this activity.

This activity will help your child talk about a variety of topics beyond their own interests. Many children with autism have special interests in particular topics or objects. Whether it's computers, dinosaurs, or traffic lights, these interests are often all they want to play with, learn about, and talk about with others. Focusing on one subject or on collecting these items can give children with autism a sense of comfort and predictability when they're faced with social interactions they feel apprehensive about.

This is a great activity to use while on the go, as it requires no materials. Give your child a topic such as "animals" and take turns naming animals as you go through the letters in the alphabet. For example, *A*—alligator, *B*—bear, and *C*—cat. As your child progresses, give them more challenging and complex topics. An alternative way to participate in this activity would be to ask your child to name as many fruits, vehicles, or pieces of clothing as they can think of. This will expand their vocabulary into many different topics. As you can see, this is a great game to play in the car with the whole family.

When this skill is mastered, expand into a conversation on a specific topic of your choosing for two exchanges, then four, then six. A *conversational exchange* is when one person speaks and another person responds with either an on-topic comment or a relevant question. You can initiate this by asking your child to name some features of an object. For example, when you ask your child about an alligator, they might mention that it has scales, has many teeth, and swims in the water. Then, begin to teach your child to ask and answer questions like "Do you think alligators make good pets?" When your child is answering, ask them to expand by explaining why they think an alligator would be a good or a bad pet. Your child will also need to take a turn coming up with a question to ask you. Steadily grow your child's ability to stay on a nonpreferred topic for longer and longer amounts of time. This simple game will help broaden your child's interests!

Continued →

TOPIC TALK, CONTINUED

WHY THIS ACTIVITY WORKS

Special interests are important to nurture, as they can help a child find like-minded friends and a meaningful career as they enter adulthood. At the same time, children also need to learn to function in a world full of variety, where their favorite topic cannot always be the only topic discussed. This easy game will assist an intermediate learner in understanding what it means to stay on topic while talking with another person, even when it's not their personal favorite topic.

TIP When first starting out, engage in conversations about your child's favorite subjects to make the interaction even more enjoyable for them. Then, as they learn how to have conversations with multiple exchanges, require the subjects chosen to be of special interest to other family members or friends.

THE LISTENING HIGH FIVE

4 Years – 9 Years

WHAT YOU'LL NEED: paper and something to draw with.

"Are you listening to me?" is a common question caregivers and teachers pose to children. This isn't always because children aren't listening; instead, it's because they often don't appear to be listening. In particular, children with autism aren't always aware of the social cues that show they're being a good listener. This activity will work on your child's active listening skills and on using social cues to show others they're paying attention to what's being said.

For this activity, you'll be drawing a hand on a piece of paper. You can trace your child's hand or draw freehand. Label each finger with an action your child can do to show someone they're listening with their whole body. If your child is familiar with the list of actions a person demonstrates when they're actively listening, you may want to list only one word on each finger, such as "Facing." Alternatively, if your child is learning the behaviors of active listening for the first time, you'll want to write an entire sentence on each finger.

You can use words or sentences from this list:

- "Facing" the speaker with your body
- "Eyes" looking at the speaker
- "Nod" head in agreement with the speaker
- "Calm" body while listening
- "Comment" with on-topic responses
- "Hands" are free of distracting items
- "Mouth" is quiet while the speaker is talking

Continued →

THE LISTENING HIGH FIVE, CONTINUED

Explain to your child that you'll be telling a story. You can invent a story or take one from a book you've read. Try to tell a story that's of interest to your child. Explain to your child that their job is to show you they're listening with their whole body. Start with a very short story that is about 10 seconds long and gradually increase the length of the story as your child's ability to actively listen increases. Have your child display what this looks like to make sure they get the idea. If, during the story, you see them displaying any of the listening actions on the hand visual, mark the finger that corresponds with the listening action with a star. If all fingers have stars by the time the story is over, give your child a high five! Encourage your child to use the listening actions while they speak with others to demonstrate they're actively listening.

WHY THIS ACTIVITY WORKS

Active listening is a crucial skill for your child to have. It will allow them to gain new information, engage in conversations, and increase their ability to make friends. Practicing good listening skills using a visual aid helps a child with autism remember all that's involved to master this skill.

TIP For some children, listening with their eyes (making eye contact) feels extremely uncomfortable. If this is the case for your child, replace "eyes looking" with "eyes wide open." If your child needs to wiggle to concentrate on what's being said, possibly replace "calm body" with "brain thinking."

FACE PAINTING

4 Years – 11 Years

WHAT YOU'LL NEED: face paint, store-bought or homemade.

One creative way to increase your child's eye contact is by painting each other's faces. Imagine the smile on your child's face when it's colorfully painted to look like their favorite character or animal. While you're painting your child's face, you'll naturally be giving each other eye contact. You can offer to paint fancy eyelashes coming out from the corner of your child's eyes or make a circle of little stars around each eye. This provides even more opportunity for your child to comfortably look at your face and eyes.

If you're extra brave, give your child a chance to paint your face as well. This will create twice the opportunity for your child to practice eye contact and will also be twice as fun! Some children may not enjoy the feeling of paint on their face and hands, and you may want to opt for playing with toy glasses, noses, or masks, or just making silly faces at each other. Your child will experience silliness and laughter while practicing this crucial skill.

WHY THIS ACTIVITY WORKS
Eye contact is a foundational social skill for all children. It's necessary for success with other social skills and learning activities and essential for a child to safely interact in the world around them.

Looking at a person's face gives us many important social clues and is important to communication because it allows us to read facial expressions and lip patterns. These facial clues are often extra important for children who have difficulty learning and using language. Fun games like face painting can be used to help children with ASD feel more comfortable using eye contact.

TIP I recommend using washable paint, which can be purchased at any local craft store. Or you and your child can easily make face paint together at home by mixing cornstarch, face lotion, natural food coloring, and a dab of vegetable oil. Creating the paint yourself allows for even more enjoyable social interaction between you and your child.

SPACE BUBBLE

4 Years – 11 Years

WHAT YOU'LL NEED: child-size Hula-Hoop.

Most of us don't realize that we walk around with a bubble that surrounds us. This invisible bubble is more typically termed our "personal space." It varies in size depending on our culture and preferences and the relationship we have with the person entering it. Parents tend not to notice their young children coming into their personal space, and often invite it, as their children remain an important extension of them throughout the toddler years. However, as a child grows up, they must follow social rules around personal space. This activity is a way to teach your child increased awareness of the unspoken boundaries of personal space. They'll learn to understand the importance of personal space and the appropriate distance to keep between themselves and others.

Have your child stand inside the Hula-Hoop, holding it up around the waist. If your child has a hard time holding up the hoop, you can use yarn or ribbon to tie it over your child's shoulders, much like suspenders. The Hula-Hoop will be your child's personal space bubble. Describe to your child how to keep hoop-distance away while talking to or playing with others. Have your child move around the area bumping into furniture, walls, and other people, so they can experience the distance. Enter your child's personal space bubble and ask how it feels. Your child will likely move their head and upper body backward or motion for you to get away.

Practice different playful scenarios while having your child stand inside the hoop pretending it's a personal space bubble. When your child isn't wearing the hoop and needs a reminder to maintain a good personal space distance, ask them to imagine being back inside their bubble and to give the other person a little more space.

This is also a good opportunity to discuss how much physical contact is appropriate to have with another person. Is it okay to walk up and touch a friend's shirt because you think it's cool? Is it okay to sit in your teacher's lap without asking first? Remind your child it's not okay to cross another person's invisible bubble.

WHY THIS ACTIVITY WORKS

Taking an abstract concept and presenting it in a concrete way helps a child with autism understand it. A child who experiences what the boundaries of personal space look and feel like inside a visual and tangible hoop will be more likely to learn the idea and use it in their everyday life. Teaching children to respect the personal space of others will lead to increased social acceptance, making it easier for them to create friendships and participate in group activities.

COMPLIMENT JAR

5 Years – 10 Years

WHAT YOU'LL NEED: any type of clear jar or other container, small household items to fill the jar, and a small prize.

This activity will surely motivate your child to engage in appropriate social interactions with you, their siblings, and their friends! I'll use the example of giving compliments, although you could alter this activity to fit whatever social skills you want to see your child improve.

In this example, we will be filling the jar with cotton balls. It's a good idea to have your child help you choose the compliment prize.

STEPS TO USING THE COMPLIMENT JAR

1. Describe to your child exactly what a compliment is. Tell your child what they will need to say in order for everyone to know it's a compliment. Be as specific as possible. For example, "A compliment is something nice you say about someone else. You compliment someone to tell them something you like about them. 'I think your earrings are very pretty' is a compliment."

2. Give your child examples of what compliments sound like.

   - "Wow, that was great!"
   - "Good job!"
   - "Nice work!"
   - "I like your . . . "
   - "You're very good at . . . "

3. Have your child practice giving you a compliment in a role-play with you. During this practice, trade off giving each other compliments. Each time your child gives a compliment during practice, show them that a cotton ball will be placed into the jar.

4. Choose an activity for your child to play with you or another person.

5. Explain to your child that you'll be watching them during the activity and listening for compliments. Every time they give a compliment, you'll place one cotton ball in the jar for your child to see. Once the jar is full, your child will receive their chosen prize!

WHY THIS ACTIVITY WORKS

This method of teaching a new behavior is called a "token economy." In this example, the behavior of giving compliments is paired with the tokens (cotton balls), and the tokens are paired with a reinforcer (prize). Because you're rewarding your child for using compliments, they'll be more likely to give compliments in the future. Using a token economy is a very effective way of increasing the behaviors you want to see your child display, while at the same time teaching delayed gratification.

TIP Set your child up for success from the very start. Begin by using a small jar so very few cotton balls will be needed to fill it. You can also assist your child by modeling compliments and allowing them to copy you.

CIRCLES OF FRIENDS

5 Years – 11 Years

WHAT YOU'LL NEED: a large piece of paper and something to write with.

Draw six circles, one within the other, so your paper looks like it's ready to use for target practice. Make the largest circle the entire size of the paper. Then label each circle. Label the smallest circle in the very center of the paper "me." The next largest circle will be labeled "family." Then, in order outward, label the circles "friends," "acquaintances," "community helpers," and "strangers."

Talk with your child about the different people in their life. Discuss who belongs in each circle and write the names of the people in their corresponding category. For example, write "Mom," "Grandma," "Grandpa," and any siblings' names in the "family" circle.

After filling out each circle, talk to your child about the type of greeting and social interaction that's appropriate to display with the people in each category. For example, hugs and kisses, a high five, waving, and smiling would all

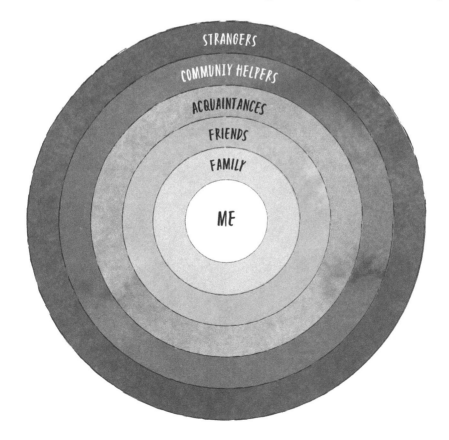

be acceptable greetings for a "family" member. Write these words in the circle labeled "family." Then, work your way outward, deciding together what type of social interactions belong with which people. Decide which greetings are suitable for your child to use with each category and teach them to differentiate between each. Give possible scenarios, such as "Who can you hug?" and have your child point to or label which categories include people they can hug. Practice this skill in your child's natural environment to see if your child can apply their knowledge when you're out in the community or visiting friends and family.

WHY THIS ACTIVITY WORKS

Greetings are a vital part of our daily lives. The ability to make a good first impression, appear approachable, and build relationships hinges on our ability to greet others proficiently. Various greetings are used throughout the day, from a *big hug to greet family members when we wake in the morning, to a verbal "Hello, how are you?" to friends and coworkers, a wave to the neighbor walking her dog, and a friendly smile to strangers passing us at the grocery store. These greetings can be a bit confusing and uncomfortable for individuals with autism. This activity will assist your child in figuring out which level of greeting is appropriate for them to use with people they encounter on a daily basis.*

TIP The Circles of Friends visual is also great to use to educate your child about important safety guidelines. You could include information like this in your circles:

- Who can you get in a car with?
- Who can help you in the bathroom?
- Who should you never keep a secret from?
- Who is it okay to tell your name and address to?

RED LIGHT, GREEN LIGHT

6 Years – 11 Years

WHAT YOU'LL NEED: paper and something to write with. Optional: homemade color cards in green, yellow, and red.

Small talk can get confusing for individuals with ASD, who often don't understand the subtle nuances of social situations. Your child may have trouble taking into account what topics are of interest to the person they are talking to, leading them to speak at length about their favorite toy or movie. This next activity is a way to help a child become socially aware when engaging with others in everyday conversations.

To start, you're going to help your child recognize the interests of others. List the names of close friends and family members on a sheet of paper, then write down what your child knows about each. For example, "Aunt Sally talks about bike riding a lot. Hmmm . . . what could you talk to her about? She might like talking about bikes, exercise, and nature."

Next, introduce your child to social cues using a street-light analogy. What clues should they

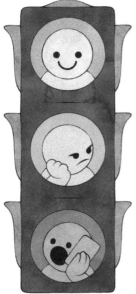

watch for when talking to others that show them the person is interested or uninterested in the topic discussed?

GREEN LIGHT ("keep talking"): smiling, nodding, making eye contact, commenting, asking questions

YELLOW LIGHT ("talk less"): looking away, checking phone, being nonresponsive

RED LIGHT ("stop talking"): beginning to walk away, answering a phone call, saying aloud they're bored or uninterested

Role-play these various indicators to see if your child picks up on the social cues and can label them by color. Hold up corresponding colored cards during actual interactions if your child needs additional support in recognizing others' interest levels.

WHY THIS ACTIVITY WORKS

This activity helps your child with perspective-taking—understanding what others are thinking and feeling—and becoming better equipped to navigate social situations. The visual aids will help your child engage in small talk that flows smoothly instead of ending in uncomfortable silence.

ACTS OF FRIENDLINESS

7 Years – 11 Years

WHAT YOU'LL NEED: nothing needed for this activity. Optional: a camera to record videos.

Most children with autism want to make and keep friends and just need a bit of extra guidance about actions that other people consider friendly. Understanding friendly and unfriendly actions will help your child make new friends. Here are some steps to assist an intermediate to advanced learner break down the concept of "friendly" into easy-to-digest parts so they have more success in creating lasting bonds with others.

1. Define these terms for your child:

    ACTS OF FRIENDLINESS: kind actions or words that make others want to be around you

    ACTS OF HURTFULNESS: harmful actions or words (either by accident or on purpose) that make others want to stay away from you

2. Give examples:

    ACTS OF FRIENDLINESS

    - Helping someone who's hurt
    - Helping someone clean up a mess
    - Complimenting someone: "That's an awesome drawing" or "You're really good at kickball"
    - Cheering for a peer
    - Smiling at peers
    - Sharing toys with peers
    - Initiating play or asking to join play with peers
    - Showing interest in what someone else is doing or talking about

    ACTS OF HURTFULNESS

    - Kicking, hitting, name calling
    - Joking about, laughing at, or criticizing someone: "You're not very good at throwing"
    - Booing or making mean faces
    - Butting into play or hogging toys

Continued →

3. **ROLE-PLAY:** Now, role-play appropriate ways to behave to make friends. You may want to make a video for your child if their body language or tone of voice needs improving, so they can see how others perceive them. For example, a child may look at the ground and mumble in a muffled voice, "Do you want to play with me?" Seeing this on camera can clue them in to making changes. In addition, recording a video of the successful friendly behavior scenarios can strengthen what it looks and sounds like in your child's mind.

4. **PRACTICE:** Challenge your child to engage in three simple acts of friendliness each day. Increase the number as they're successful and encourage them to keep trying even if they didn't get the reaction they were looking for the first time.

WHY THIS ACTIVITY WORKS

This activity helps create a clear picture of what being friendly looks and sounds like. Giving your child these small steps to perform will help them make new friends.

CHAPTER SEVEN

LET'S MOVE!

Motor skills are actions that result from the movement of muscles. Motor skills can be broken down into multiple categories, including oral motor, visual motor, fine motor, and gross motor. Oral motor skills are the movements of the muscles around the mouth. Children use oral motor skills when they chew and swallow food, blow bubbles under water, and articulate words. Visual motor skills (also called visual integration skills) allow a child to coordinate their hand movements with the use of their eyes. Children use visual motor skills when they work on a puzzle, string beads, and use scissors to cut on a dotted line. Fine motor skills are the movements of small muscles. Examples of fine motor skills typically displayed by children include buttoning clothing, pinching coins, and swiping a tablet. Gross motor skills are the movements of larger muscles, including crawling under a table, running during a game of chase, and jumping into a pool. Almost everything a child does requires motor skills.

Many children with autism don't develop motor skills at the same rate as other children. In addition, some children with ASD aren't able to learn other needed skills until they have strengthened their motor skills in multiple categories. For example, a child with autism who doesn't yet have the fine motor skills to pinch a puzzle piece may become frustrated when asked to work on a puzzle. It's possible that they would happily complete the task if they had the fine motor skill of the pincer grasp (the use of the thumb and forefinger to pick up small objects). In this case, they'll need to be taught the pincer grasp before being expected to independently complete a puzzle. In the meantime, the child will need hand-over-hand help to pick up and manipulate each puzzle piece.

Strengthening your child's motor skills is very important and is something you can practice at home. Most ABA programs teach motor skills with the same strategies used to teach any other skill. Your child will need your physical assistance in the beginning for these activities. Over time, you'll want to gradually fade the level of help you provide as your child's muscles strengthen and their visual coordination increases. Eventually your child will be able to perform these motor skills independently. Along the way, it's important to praise and reward your child for their efforts in practicing these skills. Learning motor skills can be very fun, as you'll discover in the following activities.

HEAD, SHOULDERS, KNEES, AND TOES

1 Year – 5 Years

WHAT YOU'LL NEED: the song "Head, Shoulders, Knees, and Toes." (You can easily find this online.)

Here's a very simple activity using a classic children's song. With this song you can teach your child the motor task of identifying parts of their body while they stretch and move in all directions. This is designed for early learners who need to develop more body-awareness skills, but this activity can be fun to do with children at any age level.

It would be best for you to sing "Head, Shoulders, Knees, and Toes" versus using a recording of the song, because then you can manipulate the song, such as slowing down or speeding up the pace, to fit your child's needs.

Begin by singing the song a few times all the way through while you demonstrate how to touch each body part as it's mentioned in the song. Next, using hand-over-hand assistance, prompt your child to touch or point to their body parts. Gradually, see if you can begin to fade your prompts as your child develops the ability to identify and touch their body parts independently.

If there's a particular body part your child is struggling to find, repeat that word in the song several times. For example, "head, head, head, shoulders, knees, and toes." Add additional body parts, such as teeth and elbows, so your child acquires an even bigger repertoire.

WHY THIS ACTIVITY WORKS
This activity achieves the goal of bringing more motor awareness to your child as they identify various parts of their body. It also involves many social interactions for your child to practice making eye contact, imitation, and communication skills.

CRISSCROSS

1 Year – 6 Years

WHAT YOU'LL NEED: a ball big enough that your child will need both hands to pick it up.

For this activity, you'll be helping your child develop the part of their brain called the *corpus callosum*—a large bundle of fibers along the middle of the brain that allows one hemisphere of the brain to communicate with the other. Gross motor activities called *crossing the midline*—the movement of reaching across the center of one's own body with an arm or a leg—give the brain practice in sharing information between the two sides.

Sit your child on the floor and roll the ball to one side of them and then the other. See if you can get your child to reach across their body to retrieve the ball with both hands.

To do this activity with a young child, you can have them sit back to back with you. Then, while twisting your torso, hand the ball off with both hands from one side to the other. You can turn this exercise into a speedy game and count with your child how many passes you do without dropping the ball. The goal is to get your child to cross the invisible line down the center of their body with both hands or legs on both sides; this will in turn grow and strengthen new pathways in their brain.

WHY THIS ACTIVITY WORKS

Children with autism often don't show the ability to cross their body midline. For example, when a child reaches their right arm way over to the left side of the table to pick up a puzzle piece, their arm has likely crossed the middle part of body and they've crossed the midline. If your child is unable to easily do this, they may lack bilateral coordination (both sides of the body working in unison). Developing your child's ability to cross the midline by engaging in this simple activity will improve this coordination.

TUNNEL FOR THE TRUNK

1 Year – 11 Years

WHAT YOU'LL NEED: a play tunnel, store-bought or homemade.

Tummy time strengthens a child's neck, back, and shoulder muscles, which is needed for them to meet their infant developmental milestones, such as sitting up, crawling, and walking. The tummy time position—in which a child lies flat on their stomach, while propping themselves up on their elbows—is especially important for a child with autism to practice, as their trunk muscles tend to need strengthening. Luckily, all people, no matter what age, can benefit greatly from spending time in this prone position.

If you don't own a play tunnel, consider investing in one; they are lots of fun for children of all ages and help develop motor skills. Play tunnels are available at many children's stores and online. You can also make a tunnel with a few chairs lined up across from one another with blankets draped between them.

For younger children, if you make a tunnel, they'll likely enjoy playing in it. See if you can maneuver your child into the tummy time position within it and help them stay in that position by giving them a novel toy to play with or a fine motor task to complete in the position.

For older, more agile children, once your tunnel is ready, create an obstacle course with the tunnel as one of the activities. Your obstacle course can include gross motor activities, such as tossing a ball, balancing, jumping, and climbing. When your child reaches the tunnel, you'll want to show them how to go through it in an "army crawl" position. This means lying on their tummy and moving themselves forward using their forearms directly in front of their body.

WHY THIS ACTIVITY WORKS
Tummy time works to strengthen trunk muscles and stimulate the brain stem, and it helps regulate the sensory processing system.

TIP It's a good idea to have your child spend 20 to 30 minutes a day in this prone position. If all else fails in getting them to remain still, try setting them up to watch their favorite show while doing tummy time. If they get up, the show goes off. When they get back into the tummy time position, turn the show back on.

GIVE ME A HAND

2 Years – 11 Years

WHAT YOU'LL NEED: common things from around the home. Optional: images of household chores.

Many of the daily chores you perform to keep your house in tip-top shape are also fantastic hand and grip workouts and a great way to connect with your child.

Here are five chores your child can help you with around the house while improving their hand strength.

CLEANING MIRRORS AND WINDOWS: Have your child crumple newspaper—if they can do it with one hand, even better. Give them a small plastic spray bottle to practice squirting on the glass. Wipe it clean. Trade off who gets to squirt the bottle and who gets to use the newspaper to clean the glass.

CLEANING COUNTERTOPS: Have your child squeeze water out of a sponge or wring out a small wet towel. Wipe the table clean. Trade off who gets to squeeze the sponge and who gets to wipe the counter.

WASHING DISHES: Put a little bit of soap in a small soap bottle so your child is forced to squeeze it strongly to get the soap onto a dish brush. Have your child scrub and rinse their own indestructible set of dishes. Take turns with each dish, which will give your child a model of how to clean each type of dishware as well as a short break between each dish they clean.

DOING LAUNDRY: Do the laundry together. Have your child carry the laundry basket, measure the detergent and pour it in, put in and take out clothes from the washer and dryer, squeeze clothespins to hang delicates, or fold their clothes, especially making balls with matching socks.

SWEEPING: Get a broom to fit your child's height and have them work on gripping it and sweeping crumbs into a dustpan. Model sweeping with a full-size broom. Ask your child to follow you and try to sweep any crumbs left behind.

WHY THIS ACTIVITY WORKS
Children with ASD tend to have low muscle tone in their hands, causing weakness when performing everyday tasks. These activities will address this directly by providing actions that can be performed on a daily basis to strengthen multiple muscles.

TIP Choose a few daily chores for your child to do. Provide a checklist that includes the name and an image of the chore to be done. Children with autism benefit greatly from visual supports, which help them understand what's expected and allow them to transition more smoothly from one activity to the next.

RAISIN RACE

3 Years – 6 Years

WHAT YOU'LL NEED: tweezers, raisins (or other tiny treats), and two bowls.

Manipulating tweezers to pick up objects using the pincer grasp is an excellent way to work on motor skills for children with ASD who are struggling with using scissors and/or pencils for drawing and writing.

The object of the game is for your child to transfer raisins from one bowl into the other, using tweezers. They'll try to transfer as many raisins as they can in the time allocated (usually 30 seconds to 2 minutes). You can place the two bowls side by side on a table, or to make this more challenging, have your child transfer raisins from a bowl on the table to a bowl placed on the other side of the room. If your child isn't fond of raisins alone, try chocolate chips, chocolate-covered raisins, cereal, or nuts. As your child improves their dexterity, have them use tongs or chopsticks, and switch from raisins to smaller foods like rice or seeds. You can also have your child try to pick up two or three food items at a time.

WHY THIS ACTIVITY WORKS

Repeated practice is an ideal way to master fine motor tasks, and these activities will certainly allow for this. In addition to developing the small muscles in the hand, exercises using tweezers work on shoulder and elbow stability, as well as hand-eye coordination. Using food treats adds to the motivation of this game.

TIP To teach a child to maneuver tweezers, have them practice the motion of touching fingers to thumb, as you would do when making a hand puppet talk. Then, show them how to hold the tweezers in the hand-puppet position. Your child may need hand-over-hand assistance when starting to practice these actions.

PAINTER'S TAPE

3 Years – 8 Years

WHAT YOU'LL NEED: a roll of painter's tape, a ballpoint pen, and an open space with hard floors or low carpeting.

Painter's tape or masking tape is an excellent tool to use indoors to target and increase gross motor skills with your child on cold and rainy days. Jumping is just one of the gross motor skills you can practice with your child using tape.

Use tape to make several lines on the floor about three feet long and one foot apart from one another. Create a starting point and label each line in numerical order (1st, 2nd, 3rd, etc.). Keep track of which line your child can jump to and challenge them to jump even farther next time around using the following ideas. You may want to model these jumping exercises for your child so they're more aware of what each looks like.

LONG JUMP: Have your child stand on the starting point and jump as far as they can. Then they can try variations: feet together, feet apart, leaping with one foot forward, swinging arms, and arms stationary.

RUNNING JUMP: Have them take a running start to see if they can make it even farther down the lines.

HOPPING JUMP: Can your child hop? Practice hopping forward on one leg from one line to the next. Be sure to have them alternate feet.

TWO-PERSON JUMP: Step together, then try jumping together with your child to see how far you can go.

WHY THIS ACTIVITY WORKS
Children typically begin to learn to jump by the time they're three years old. For children with autism, gross motor skills are often delayed by six months or more. These activities will help your child gain assurance with jumping so they can be more sure-footed when participating with their peers on the playground.

TIP Another option is to make small squares with tape scattered around the room and have your child jump in different arrangements from one square to the other. Make it a game of "don't step out of the square or you'll get gobbled up by the square monster," with the square monster played by Mom or Dad!

BALANCING BONANZA

3 Years – 11 Years

WHAT YOU'LL NEED: index cards, a pen, a spoon, and a small item (a cotton ball, piece of pasta, or tiny building block).

Here's a game that's sure to make balancing practice a lot more entertaining. It will test your child's ability to remain stable while maneuvering an object on a spoon in several different ways.

On index cards, write out the actions you and your child will do while holding an item on a spoon in your hand (or, for more advanced contestants, on a spoon in your mouth).

EXAMPLE BALANCING ACTIONS:

- Stand on one foot
- Walk backwards
- Walk in a line heel to toe
- Sidestep
- Transfer the item from bowl to bowl
- Move from a seated to standing position with no hands for support
- Jump in place
- Twist left to right
- Touch elbow of hand holding the spoon to the opposite knee
- Bear walk or crab crawl with spoon in the mouth

Take turns picking a card and reading what the balancing act will be. If the player who picks the card successfully performs the action without dropping the item on the spoon, the player keeps the card. If the player performs the action but drops the item off the spoon, the opponent gets a turn attempting the same balancing act. If they're successful, they'll earn the card. If they're not successful, it's your child's or another player's turn. Continue until all cards have been drawn and actions have been performed successfully. The player with the most cards at the end of the game is the winner!

WHY THIS ACTIVITY WORKS

Children with autism often struggle with lack of coordination, sometimes appearing almost clumsy. A lack of balance plays a key role in this difficulty organizing their movements and also affects their ability to develop advanced skills, such as hopping, skipping, galloping, and riding a bike. This activity allows them to practice balancing at various levels of difficulty.

ART FOR ALL

3 Years – 11 Years

WHAT YOU'LL NEED: a large piece of kraft paper, crayons, scissors, and any other art supplies you have around.

Through art, children can explore the world around them and the deep, dynamic inner world of themselves. There are so many ways that art benefits children, especially those with autism. For this activity, we'll focus on the fine motor aspect of art. Here is just one of many art projects you can do with your child, at any age, to work on their fine motor development.

1. Have your child trace the entire outline of your body on the paper. If you child has no experience with this, show them how it's done by having them practice tracing their hand on a sheet of paper. To help them to use the proper grip, give them a small broken crayon to trace with. This is also a great activity for visual motor integration, because your child will be coordinating their eyes and hands in completing a task.

2. Next, your child will get to decorate the body outline in any way they choose. Beginner learners may just be exploring colors and textures. They can paint with a brush abstractly or add features to the body, working on their grip and drawing shapes. Older, more advanced learners may choose to draw more intricate features of a body, creating a science project to learn the organs of the body.

3. Have your child help you cut out the work of art and hang it in your child's room. Cutting works on coordination of both sides of the body, visual motor integration, finger dexterity, and much more.

WHY THIS ACTIVITY WORKS

No matter what art activity you do with your child, whether it's simply coloring a picture or creating an elaborate mural, fine motor skills are in action and improving. Art projects like this strengthen core motor skills along with sensory input, focus, and collaboration with others.

TIP Try not to control the activity too much. Instead, let your child explore the art materials and see what ideas they come up with. Be creative, get messy, and have a blast!

PIZZA, PIZZA!

4 Years – 7 Years

WHAT YOU'LL NEED: store-bought or home-made play dough, and small, hard objects such as pennies, pegs, or beads. (Note: Dough and small objects can be tempting for young children to put in their mouths, so close supervision is needed.)

Here's an activity that's sure to be a hit! You'll make a play-dough pizza and give your child a ton of practice with fine motor skills. You should make a mini pizza at the same time so you can model the steps for your learner as you go.

The first two actions practice *bilateral coordination*, organizing the use of both sides of the body at the same time to complete a task.

STEP 1: Have your child roll their pizza dough into a ball between their two hands.

STEP 2: Have your child then flatten out the pizza dough by pounding it down with two hands.

The next actions work on the *pincer grasp*, picking up small items with thumb and forefinger.

STEP 3: Scatter the pennies, pegs, or beads on the table and have your child pick them up using their pincer grasp, and then push them one by one into the pizza dough as if they're the sauce and cheese on the pizza.

STEP 4: Assist your child in making the toppings by rolling small pieces of dough into balls using only their tripod fingers (the thumb, index, and middle fingers). Then place them on top of the pizza. This tripod finger exercise will develop the arch over the knuckles, called the *distal transverse metacarpal arch.*

STEP 5: There's one last fine motor activity for your child to do, which they'll likely enjoy the most. Smoosh the dough into a big ball again. Now ask your child to find the small objects still hidden inside. They'll once again need to use these pincer grasp and some very fine motor movements to remove these items from the ball of dough.

WHY THIS ACTIVITY WORKS
This pizza-making activity works on strengthening the muscles and joints in your child's hands as well as improving finger coordination and grasp. Additionally, these are all great exercises to improve handwriting skills!

CRAB CRAWL

5 Years – 11 Years

WHAT YOU'LL NEED: nothing needed for this activity. Optional: a timer.

Here comes a humongous elephant! Watch out for that crouching tiger! I see a slithering snake! It's a jungle in here! Moving like animals is a great opportunity to engage in pretend play. It's also exceptionally fun gross motor practice for your young ones. In particular, the crab crawl works on a gamut of muscles that our kiddos need to strengthen.

HOW TO DO A CRAB CRAWL

1. Have your child sit down on the floor with their feet firmly on the ground, knees bent.

2. Place their arms so they're behind the hips, palms flat on the ground.

3. Show your child how to lift their hips and midsection off the ground.

4. Assist your child in moving forward or backward on hands and feet, one step at a time.

You may want to have crab races or use a timer to keep track of your child's progress.

Once your child has gotten the hang of how to move this way, you can teach them more advanced crab crawl movements. While your child is in the crab crawl position, place an item on their stomach and see if they can move from one room to the other without dropping it. Try giving your child obstacles and different terrains to conquer while being a crab. Better yet, try doing a crabby dance by lifting one hand or leg.

WHY THIS ACTIVITY WORKS

The crab crawl is an exercise that requires no external equipment and works so many areas in the body that children with ASD need to strengthen. The crab crawl will improve arm and leg strength, motor control, body awareness, core muscles, trunk stability, and overall cardiovascular health.

TIP The crab crawl can be a challenging exercise for a child with low muscle tone. Take it slow, starting with only getting into the crab crawl position the first day, then taking one or two steps forward as your child is ready. The more your child practices this exercise, even if only for a few minutes a day, the more muscle memory they'll build.

CHAPTER EIGHT

LET'S GET SENSORY SMART!

ensory integration is a neurological process that regulates a person's sensations of their own body coming into contact with the environment. A person's sensory integration allows them to feel the breeze as a soft tickle on the skin, hear a siren as an ambulance zooms by, and see the print on a billboard from 500 feet away.

Children with ASD are sometimes described as being under sensitive and other times described as overly sensitive. One child may be highly sensitive to noise, requiring earmuffs to attend a sporting event because of all the loud cheering. Another child might have low visual sensitivities and would benefit from large print and bigger pictures when participating in an academic task. As a parent of a child with autism, you've likely noticed some special sensory sensitivities in your child. It's common for children with autism to find the processing of sensory information a challenge. The unique way these children process their environment can sometimes result in them finding ordinary situations very uncomfortable.

A child who's highly sensitive to sound may not be able to sleep through the night. A child who's overly sensitive to touch may have difficulty wearing clothing with itchy tags. A child who's extra sensitive to bright light may not be able to tolerate sitting under the fluorescent bulbs in the classroom. Engaging in sensory integration activities throughout the day can alleviate some of these sensitivities, allowing children with ASD to feel more comfortable.

Occupational therapy, provided by a licensed professional, often includes activities that are designed to meet a child's sensory needs to help the child feel more comfortable with the way their body feels when coming in contact with the surrounding environment. A list of scheduled sensory integration activities that a child engages throughout each day is often called a "sensory diet." Creating a rich variety of sensory activities for your child to engage in morning, noon, and night will undoubtedly make your child more comfortable with their body and prepared to face daily tasks. The activities in this chapter give you a variety of options to choose from when creating a personal sensory diet for your child. You'll also learn that, in addition to the activities given here, there are numerous opportunities all around you to help your child with sensory integration. Try all the following activities to find the ones your child enjoys most. Then, add these activities to your daily routine and watch your child's aversions and sensitivities slowly diminish, increasing their comfort level with the world around them. Consult with a qualified specialist, such as an occupational therapist (OT), for additional therapeutic advice and treatment options.

THE HUMAN BURRITO

1 Year – 8 Years

WHAT YOU'LL NEED: a blanket or sheet.

This deep-pressure activity works magically for children who seem to be moving around constantly and are sometimes described as "hyperactive." Too much noise, movement, and excitement can quickly cause a child with autism to become overstimulated. If you notice your child is headed in this direction, it's the perfect time to take them aside to a quiet environment where you can . . . turn them into a burrito!

Introduce your child to this activity when they're completely calm. If your child enjoys being in this restraining and increased state of bodily pressure, you can use this fun exercise when you see behavior patterns escalating and becoming hyper or agitated.

1. Take your child into an area of your home where you won't be disturbed. Tell your child you'll be wrapping them up like a burrito. (You may first need to explain what a burrito is.)

2. Wrap them tightly in a blanket or sheet, paying particular attention to head, legs, and feet.

3. If your child appears to need even more deep pressure, you can lay your body across theirs or give them additional squeezes while they're wrapped up.

4. To make this activity extra enjoyable for your child, tell them with each roll what ingredients you will be adding to their burrito. Pretend to put in cheese, rice, and beans, while keeping your voice low and calm.

WHY THIS ACTIVITY WORKS

Scientific evidence supports the idea that deep pressure has positive effects on the autonomic nervous system—the body's control system, which regulates breathing, heartbeat, blood flow, and other body functions. In particular, the act of wrapping the body up tightly (much like you swaddle an infant) gives a child with ASD, who may be overstimulated, a soothing feeling and sense of security.

SENSORY CRAVER

1 Year – 11 Years

WHAT YOU'LL NEED: your choice of clay or putty, gum, pillows, music, and balloons.

The brains of sensory-seeking children seem to crave intense sensory input. When your child is seeking out sensory experiences, you may observe them attempting to eat nonfood objects, excessively bumping into others, making nonfunctional noises with their mouth, or possibly engaging in self-injurious behaviors. Developing a sensory diet that incorporates the intense, but appropriate, activities they desire can calm their bodies.

Here are some activities you can do at home to help your sensory seeker self-regulate:

CLAY OR PUTTY: Press on it, pull it apart, and roll it between their hands. This gives your child the tactile input they need.

CHEWING: Give your child gum to chew, or buy a chewy toy for children. These toys come in an array of textures and formats.

FREEZE DANCE: Turn up the music and let your child go wild. When the music stops, have them freeze in place.

PILLOW FIGHT: If your child loves bumping and crashing into things, they'll love to be knocked over and fall on pillows.

YOGA: Child yoga poses are a great way to give your child deep pressure and stretch their joints. Those seeking *vestibular input* (related to the inner ear and body movement/position) will love trying a headstand against the wall with your support.

BALLOON BATTING: Play "keep the balloon off the floor" using your hands or a pool noodle. This will get your child jumping and moving as well as supply them with visual input.

WHY THIS ACTIVITY WORKS

If you have a sensory-seeking child, bodily challenges can increase their frustration with the world around them, interfering with the ability to develop meaningful relationships and participate in group or classroom settings. These activities give your child a dose of the sensory input they need to be better able to handle everyday interactions and tasks.

TIP Incorporate a sensory diet that's scheduled to begin before crucial focus times of the day when your child needs to pay attention. For example, engage in sensory integration activities before tackling seated school assignments, eating a meal, or settling down at bedtime.

SOUND SENSITIVITIES

1 Year – 11 Years

WHAT YOU'LL NEED: things that make sounds your child doesn't like; videos, sound recordings, or images of the sounds; and small rewards.

Many children with autism are highly sensitive to certain everyday sounds. Sensory-processing issues related to sounds your child finds aversive may lead to the development of a fear of the sound. This may cause your child to want to avoid the sound at all costs by running off when they hear it, covering their ears, or having a meltdown. In essence, your child is experiencing "sensory overload." By gradually exposing your child to the sounds that bother them, you can help your child become desensitized to those sounds. Try out this process to help your sound-sensitive kiddo.

I'll use the example of a child who has sensitivity to the sound of a baby crying. When participating in this activity with your child, replace the sound of a baby crying with whatever sounds your child is sensitive to.

1. Slowly introduce your child to babies through books and toy baby dolls. Use materials that are small, quiet, and not overly agitating to your child. Read books with a baby in the story, and use baby dolls in creative, fun ways within pretend play.

2. After you've started with only happy baby play, gradually insert some moderate and then eventually louder crying sounds you could make with your own mouth.

3. Next, find images of a baby crying and show them to your child. Make silly crying expressions and sounds together.

4. Show your child videos of children crying; start on mute, and gradually increase the volume and amount of time exposed to the sound.

5. Once your child is okay tolerating listening to the baby cry on a video, find a relative or friend with a baby you can visit to expose your child to the more sudden onset of a crying baby.

This process can go as quickly or slowly as you see fit for your child. Most important, always remember to positively reinforce your child for all baby exposure with highly rewarding items and activities. Use praise and other valuable prizes throughout all the steps in this activity, except when your child displays negative behaviors such as whining, crying, or running off.

Continued →

SOUND SENSITIVITES, CONTINUED

WHY THIS ACTIVITY WORKS

Children with ASD often have sensory processing difficulties that affect their ability to enjoy their everyday lives. Through this gradual desensitization, you can diminish your child's sensitivity to aversions in their environment, improving the life of your child and family. Systematic desensitization is a well-established and proven behavioral method to treat fear, anxiety, and phobias.

TIP Use noise-canceling headphones with caution. They can be a successful solution and are sometimes necessary to alleviate your child's anxiety. But if headphones are overused without helping your child to learn to tolerate a variety of sounds, they may be reliant on them for much longer than necessary.

TRAMPOLINE FRENZY

3 Years – 11 Years

WHAT YOU'LL NEED: a mini or full-size trampoline, a variety of flash cards, a soft ball, plush toys, and music.

Many children with ASD absolutely love jumping on trampolines. Why wouldn't they? It's a great source of sensory stimulation on many levels. Here are some ideas for how to make the most of the time your child spends jumping on their trampoline. These activities can be used with a mini or a large trampoline. A word of caution: Trampolines can be hazardous, especially without proper supervision. Be vigilant when your child jumps on a trampoline and *always* supervise.

JUMPING ACADEMICS: Practice basic academic tasks while your child jumps in front of you. For younger children, it may be as simple as saying their ABCs or bringing out the flash cards to label colors, letters, or numbers. For older children, you can encourage them to count by three, six, or nine; state math facts; or practice their list of spelling words for the week.

DODGEBALL: Slowly throw a very soft ball toward your child and have them practice dodging it. This is a great way to improve balance and coordination.

TOY BOUNCE: Place several stuffed toys on the trampoline and challenge your child to jump high enough to bounce them all off the island (trampoline) and into the lava (floor).

Continued →

DANCE-OFF: Play music and encourage your child to show off their craziest dance moves, run in place, jump with coordinated arm moves, and jump side to side.

WHY THIS ACTIVITY WORKS

Trampolines are excellent to use first thing in the morning with children who tend to have low energy and are under-responsive to their sensory environment. This helps wake up their body and get ready to start their day. It's also great to incorporate into a sensory diet at various intervals throughout the day. Trampolining is a terrific alternative to organized sports as a way for your child to get the benefits of exercise. It helps your child gain control of their whole body in motion while balancing and jumping.

TIP If you don't own a trampoline, your child will still have tons of fun and benefit from participating in jumping academics, dodgeball, and the dance-off played right on your living room floor!

GREAT BALL OF JOY

3 Years – 11 Years

WHAT YOU'LL NEED: a large exercise ball. Optional: music and a simple activity like beading.

Large exercise balls are a low-cost resource you can use to do numerous sensory integration activities with your child that they'll love. Exercise balls can help a child rev up their energy if they're understimulated or bring their energy level down if they're overstimulated. Here are some examples of activities you can use at home to support your child's sensory needs.

BOUNCING ON THE BALL: If you want to calm your child down, have them sit on the ball as though it's a chair and do small up-and-down bounces and side-to-side wiggles. Your child may need a helping hand to stay balanced while bouncing. Give your child a quiet activity to do while sitting on the ball, such as squeezing a squishy ball, completing a fine motor task of stringing beads, or playing soft music. If you want your child to be more alert and attentive, have them bounce higher, possibly while sitting in your lap. You can also have them bounce on the ball while scooting across the room.

BALL PLAY: Playing with your big ball is not only fun, but also great heavy work and a visual perception exercise. Have your child try dribbling the ball on the ground, throwing it against the wall and catching it, or kicking it across the grass. Bounce soft items off the ball and see if your child can track them with their eyes and point out where they land.

THE ROLL OVER: Have your child lie on the ground facedown and roll the ball over them. Apply pressure to all areas of their body. Ask your child or watch their facial expression to see if they want you to apply more or less pressure. Have your child tell you the body parts where they want more pressure added. This is a great way to encourage communication while meeting sensory needs.

WHY THIS ACTIVITY WORKS

Exercise is an evidence-based practice that has been proven to decrease self-stimulatory and repetitive behavior patterns in children with autism. These simple exercise activities provide your child with an array of sensory input that helps minimize their need to engage in stereotypical behaviors, become hyperactive, or act aggressively. The exercise ball can be incorporated into your child's everyday routine as part of their sensory diet.

SENSORY NATURE WALK

3 Years – 11 Years

WHAT YOU'LL NEED: comfortable clothes and shoes and a roll of strong tape. Optional: a hat and sunglasses.

Being with nature enriches the lives of children. The sensory experience we receive while being outdoors is only one of the many gifts nature gives us. A sensory nature walk is beneficial to individuals who need to calm or heighten their senses. Whether you're able to get outside in the backyard or a neighborhood park, or you have access to a beach or the luxury of walking on a lush forest trail, you'll never regret trading screen time for serene time.

FOR CHILDREN WHO ARE UNDERSTIMU-LATED BY THEIR ENVIRONMENT

If it's safe to do so, consider having your child go on the nature walk barefoot. This will improve their senses beneath their feet. Wake up your child's nervous system with some time to stretch, run, jump, or climb at the beginning of your walk. Bring a roll of packing tape you can wrap around your child's hand with the sticky side up. Your child can use this to collect various artifacts from nature, such as small rocks, sticks, leaves, and feathers. When they find an artifact, use this valuable opportunity to talk about it. How does it feel? Have your child crunch

the leaves beneath their feet, smoosh the soil or mud between their fingers, feel the sunshine or wind on their face, smell the wildflowers, close their eyes, and name the sounds they hear around them.

FOR CHILDREN WHO ARE OVERSTIMU-LATED BY THEIR ENVIRONMENT:
Sometimes children can become overwhelmed with too much stimulation in their environment. If this sounds like your child, a nature walk can help expose them to sensory experiences in a slow and soothing fashion. Make sure to give them a hat to block out the bright sun; also make sure they wear comfortable clothing and shoes. Start by taking them to a quiet place without a lot of distractions, like busy streets and road noise, for a short time. Then, gradually increase the length of time and their exposure to the sensory experiences around them.

WHY THIS ACTIVITY WORKS
Nature is truly healing for children with autism. It's a great form of sensory integration therapy to assist in processing their world, and it also develops creativity, cognitive skills, and social relationships and relieves stress. This is true for all of us!

TERRIFIC TASTINGS

3 Years – 11 Years

WHAT YOU'LL NEED: two game pieces, a die, two sheets of paper, a special food reward, and the food you would like to teach your child to eat.

A common challenge caregivers face raising a child with autism is the daily task of eating. Your child may experience *sensory food aversion*—food refusal, gagging, and tantrum behaviors at mealtimes as they struggle to process the sensory experience that comes with the appearance, texture, smell, or taste of certain foods. This game will help you introduce your child to new foods to slowly build their repertoire of preferred foods.

NOTE: Seek advice from a qualified specialist, such as an occupational therapist, for additional treatment options. Simply playing "Terrific Tastings" will not be enough support for severe or diagnosed feeding issues.

CREATING THE GAME

Draw eight squares on both pieces of paper. Inside the squares, write the following, in the following order:

LEVEL 1: "Look" (at food)

LEVEL 2: "Touch" (with finger)

LEVEL 3: "Hold" (in hand)

LEVEL 4: "Smell" (the food)

LEVEL 5: "Kiss" (the food)

LEVEL 6: "Mouth 5 seconds" (hold in mouth)

LEVEL 7: "Mouth 25 seconds"
(hold in mouth)

LEVEL 8: "Chew and Swallow" (the food)

PLAYING THE GAME

1. Place your child's coveted food reward in a bowl in the middle of the table.

2. Sit at the table across from your child, with a sheet of paper in front of each of you.

3. Place a small amount of the new tasting food on plates and keep them nearby.

4. Take turns rolling the die to perform the correlating number of levels with the tasting food. For example, if your child rolls a 2 at the beginning of the game, they must perform Level 1 and Level 2 before moving the game piece to square 2.

5. Move the game piece the number of squares indicated. (If a player doesn't want to do both moves, they can pass on their turn, and the partner gets to roll.)

The first player to make it to Level 8 wins the reward food! Play for only a short time (5 to 10 minutes) so you end the game on a positive note, and praise your child for their efforts.

WHY THIS ACTIVITY WORKS
This activity is a playful way to reduce the anxiety your child may feel around mealtime. Slow exposure to a sensory experience is a proven method to help with desensitization and tolerance.

LITTLE YOGIS

3 Years – 11 Years

WHAT YOU'LL NEED: gym mat or towel, and comfortable clothes.

Yoga practice, when done regularly, can improve your child's sensory processing and integration. Here are just a few yoga poses to get your child started! The Kids Yoga Stories website has some additional great examples. (See the listing in the Resources section on page 158.)

You'll want a quiet location for this activity.

BUMBLE BEE BREATHING: One of the most important aspects of yoga is the breath. Begin your yoga practice by having your child sit cross-legged on the floor with their hands in their lap or in prayer position at their heart. Show them how to inhale through their nose and, when exhaling, create a humming bee noise in their throat. This calms their nervous system.

DOWNWARD DOG POSE: Have your child begin this pose in a crawl position with their fingers spread and palms flat on the floor. Now have them create an inverted V shape by lifting their buttocks in the air while keeping a straight back. Encourage them to keep their heels flat and look at their knees. This will provide your child with both vestibular (inner ear) and proprioceptive (joint compression/heavy work) input.

TREE POSE: Have your child stand with one foot flat against their calf or inner thigh. Start by having your child find their balance by extending their arms out to their sides into the shape of a *T*. As balancing improves, have them bring their hands into prayer position over their heart or over their head. Have them sing or count while looking at a specific item in the room to keep focused. This is great for vestibular input.

SLEEPING POSE: At the end of your yoga practice, it's nice to finish with Savasana. Have your child lie flat on the mat with their eyes closed, body quiet, and breath relaxed. This pose should be done for as long as your child can remain lying still, with a goal of 10 minutes. Sleeping pose teaches your child to go from a hyperstimulated state to a restorative state for their body organs, nervous system, and mind.

WHY THIS ACTIVITY WORKS

When your child's sensory system needs refocusing, yoga is the way to go. Give your child the added bonus of learning mindfulness, gaining strength, improving bowel functioning, and getting better sleep. Namaste!

TIP Some children will need you to physically guide their bodies into the correct pose. Older children may be able to imitate the pose as you model it for them.

SENSORY BOTTLE

5 Years – 11 Years

WHAT YOU'LL NEED: a bowl, hair gel or shampoo (the cheaper the better), warm water, a clean plastic bottle (the thicker the better), a funnel, tiny plastic toys, glitter, and strong glue or a hot glue gun.

When a child becomes overly stimulated, sometimes you want a quick, easy activity to quiet their mind and body. Sensory bottles are just the thing. There are many variations of sensory bottles, and every child has their preference for which satisfies their personal sensory needs. Here is one to try out with items you likely have around your house!

1. Working together, mix two parts hair gel with six parts warm water in the bowl. Let it cool and settle.

2. Use the funnel to pour your gel-water mixture into the plastic bottle, filling it 90 percent full.

3. Add as much glitter as you like.

4. Add 5 to 15 small plastic toys, depending on their size and your preference.

5. Add more gel-water mixture until the bottle is completely full.

6. Tighten the lid and give the bottle a few strong shakes. Watch how quickly the toys fall.

7. Not quite right? Empty the bottle contents back into the bowl.

8. Too slow? Add more warm water (let it cool), then funnel back in.

9. Too fast? Add more hair gel or shampoo (let it settle), then funnel back in.

10. Once you've got it right, dry the lid and rim, then secure the lid with glue.

WHY THIS ACTIVITY WORKS

Sensory bottles allow your child time to focus, calm their anxiety, and process their emotions. They also provide an opportunity to practice eye tracking and give your child a good dose of visual sensory input. Once you get to try it out, you just might decide you need to make one for yourself!

BIKES AND TRIKES

5 Years – 11 Years

WHAT YOU'LL NEED: a bicycle or tricycle and safety gear. Optional: training wheels.

During the practice of biking, your child will be learning a way to get around, strengthening motor skills, and gaining an activity to share with friends, all while experiencing a variety of sensory inputs.

STEP 1: Make sure your child is wearing appropriate safety gear. A properly fitted helmet is a must, and you may want to add elbow pads, kneepads, and wrist guards.

STEP 2: Have your child get to know their bike in a safe place. Set up pillows and blankets and let your child have fun getting on and off the bike, playing with the pedals, and singing songs while they sit on the bike. This is a great time to make sure the seat is the right height, so your child can firmly plant their feet on the ground, before heading outside to begin the riding lesson.

STEP 3: Take the bike outside to a safe area, free of any potential dangers, and encourage your child to walk the bike around, taking long steps, so the bike begins to roll forward. Make sure your child is comfortable gliding the bike forward with long steps and steering by turning the handlebars.

STEP 4: Help your child sit on the bike while you hold the bike up by grabbing the back of the seat in one hand and the front of the handlebars in the other. Allow your child to push the pedals forward while you balance the bike. During this step, teach your child how to use the brakes and how to put their feet down if they need to stop.

STEP 5: Slowly fade the amount of balance you provide and begin to let them ride for brief distances without your support. Soon your child will be able to balance and pedal for longer and longer until they're riding independently!

WHY THIS ACTIVITY WORKS
Riding a bike provides your child with a variety of sensory input, from the resistance the pedals provide as your child pushes their legs forward to the feeling of the breeze brushing across their cheeks. Biking can also strengthen your child's motor planning, safety awareness, and balance.

TIP If your child doesn't yet have the ability to balance on the bike, start with a tricycle or a bike with training wheels. For a child who doesn't possess the strength to push the pedals by themselves, biking is still a great activity for them to try while you walk alongside and help push forward. Your child can practice the movements that will allow them to bike independently in the future while their muscles continue to develop.

CHAPTER NINE

LET'S GET CALM!

There isn't one simple definition for *self-regulation,* but you can think about it as your child's ability to manage their own emotions and their impulse to overreact. Put another way, a child who has strong self-regulation skills is able to stay calm during states of extreme difficultly or excitement.

Children with autism often become distressed more quickly than typical children. They can be agitated by a variety of circumstances, perhaps because of hypersensitivities or a lack of strong social skills. Combine this with underdeveloped communication and language, and your child may easily become upset without having a good method to calm down. Imagine how frustrating this may be for your child.

To have strong self-regulation skills, your child needs an array of self-soothing techniques and an awareness of how and when to implement them. The following activities are designed to teach your child a variety of calming strategies they can use when feeling upset. Some of the activities include lessons created to help your child independently know when to use one of their calming strategies, while others provide a visual support to use as a reminder of appropriate options when anxieties are high. All of the activities are enjoyable for children and have been made especially for you and your child to do together. Participating in these activities will shed light on a diverse set of tools your child can use to calm down. Together, the two of you will be able to choose the best ones to pull out of your toolbox when it's time.

HELPING HAND

2 Years – 5 Years

WHAT YOU'LL NEED: a clear container that's hard to open and a favorite toy or a special treat that fits inside.

Difficulty performing a task can often be the cause of a great deal of anguish and strife for a child with ASD. This stress can lead to needless problem behaviors. Teaching your child how and when to ask for help frees them from feeling helpless and gives them a way to become self-reliant.

TEACHING YOUR CHILD HOW TO ASK FOR HELP

Here's a way to encourage a beginner learner to ask for assistance. Enclose the toy or treat in the container and offer the container to your child. If the item inside is of value to your child, they'll likely attempt to open it. At that point, immediately prompt them to ask for help in any way they can. Accept all responses, whether your child uses sign language, the *h* sound, the single word "help," or more complex language. Then quickly open the container so they can retrieve the reward. Continue to do this activity until your child can ask you for help independently. Vary the arrangement, setting, and people involved in this activity in order to generalize the skill.

TEACHING YOUR CHILD WHEN TO ASK FOR HELP

Using a social script is a great way to teach your child when it's appropriate to ask for help. Read the social script just prior to a time when you know your child may need assistance.

Here's an example:

Sometimes a task like putting together a toy or finishing my homework can be hard.

I may need help from my mom to complete the task.

I can ask for help by using my words.

I'll wait quietly until my mom comes to help me.

My mom is happy, and I feel good when I ask for the help I need.

WHY THIS ACTIVITY WORKS

These activities involve teaching your child to use functional communication *to request help independently. Functional Communication Training (FCT) is an evidence-based practice for teaching children with autism. These are also proactive strategies that reduce the likelihood of a problem behavior occurring.*

ROARING LION

3 Years – 8 Years

WHAT YOU'LL NEED: a small toy or stuffed animal. Optional: a picture of a lion roaring.

Focused breathing during stressful times is a critical skill to teach children with ASD so they're equipped to self-regulate their emotions and bring themselves back to a place of calm. Here are a few fun breathing techniques that will benefit your child.

LION ROAR BREATHING
Show your child how to interlock their fingers under their chin. Have them inhale through their nose, while they raise their elbows so their hands frame their face. On the exhale, have them roar quietly like a lion out of their mouth while they bring their elbows back down to their chest. Have them do this five times. You can give them an image of a roaring lion to help them remember how to exhale.

BIRTHDAY CANDLE BREATHING
Have your child hold up five fingers to represent five candles on a birthday cake. Ask them to take a deep breath, imagining they're smelling the flavor of their favorite cake, then blow the first candle (finger) out. Each time they blow, they'll bend down one finger until their hand is in a fist.

BELLY BREATHING
Have your child lie down on their back. Tell them they'll be breathing in and out through their tummy. To help them remember to use their stomach to breathe, place a small, lightweight toy or stuffed animal on their stomach and have them try to make it move up and down while they breathe. Once they've mastered belly breathing while lying down, transition to sitting in a chair.

WHY THIS ACTIVITY WORKS
Concentrated breathing benefits children with autism by giving them an effective way to respond to stress both psychologically and physically. Using breathing techniques along with guided visualization can enhance their ability to focus on their breathing.

PATIENCE, MY FRIEND

3 Years – 8 Years

WHAT YOU'LL NEED: an index card, a red pen or marker, and a visual timer. Optional: a small special treat.

Waiting. Children are certainly expected to do a lot of it. Children wait for their turn to go down the slide, their teacher to dismiss them for recess, and their sibling to put down their favorite toy. For many children, waiting is confusing and can feel like it takes *forever*. For children with autism, having to wait can sometimes escalate to severe meltdowns. So, how can you teach your child with autism to master the art of waiting? This game will help. The more practice your child has performing this life skill, the stronger their self-regulation skills will be when it comes to waiting. Remember to make this game fun by keeping the wait time short. You'll want your child to be successful almost every time. Also, remember to praise and reward your child when they wait appropriately and win the round. They'll want to play over and over!

1. Write "wait" in red on an index card to create a "Wait Card."

2. Figure out how long your child can wait for a preferred toy or activity without engaging in problem behaviors. If it's only 30 seconds, no problem. Start this activity with a 10-second goal so your child will be successful right off the bat.

3. Select a moderately preferred item for your child to practice waiting for—for example, a blue marker if your child sometimes likes to draw.

4. Sit your child down and explain they'll need to wait for 10 seconds for the item. Your child may be waiting a longer or shorter duration of time depending on the item.

5. Give your child the Wait Card to hold while they wait. Set the timer for the length of time agreed upon. When the timer beeps, immediately compliment your child by telling them, "You did it! That was amazing waiting!" Exchange the Wait Card for the item they were waiting for. Pair your praise with tickles, a high-five, or a small treat.

6. As your child is successful, steadily increase the time they're asked to wait.

7. If your child becomes agitated while waiting, it's important to refrain from giving them their item until they're calm for at least a few seconds. If your child isn't successful in the beginning, it's likely that the initial wait time was too long, so you'll want to shorten it.

8. As your child improves this skill, think about using it in the community. Soon enough, your child will learn to be patient no matter where you go and how long they need to wait.

WHY THIS ACTIVITY WORKS
Through this activity, you're steadily shaping your child's behavior using positive reinforcement. This is an evidence-based practice for children with autism and the most commonly used intervention in ABA.

TIP If you don't have a visual timer on your phone, try counting out loud together as you wait for the time to pass.

POWER UP

4 Years – 7 Years

WHAT YOU'LL NEED: paper and something to write and draw with.

Whether it's a simple card game or a physical sport, losing a game can be difficult for children with ASD. The child's lack of control over the game action and outcome often leads to frustration. In addition, games involve other people and require your child to use their social skills, which can be stressful. To curb the challenging behaviors sometimes brought about by this anxiety and to teach your child the socially appropriate expectations for being a good sport, you may need the help of a superhero! You might be asking, what do you mean by *superhero?*

STEP 1: Invent a superhero character based on your child's special interests. This could be a favorite cartoon character, animal, or movie personality.

STEP 2: Write a short script from the perspective of your child's superhero that highlights the behavior you want your child to display when they lose a game.

Here's an example for a child who loves the cartoon character Daniel Tiger:

Daniel Tiger loves playing games with his family and friends. Sometimes he wins and sometimes he loses. When he wins a game, he always feels excited! He may say, "I won" while cheering. When he loses, he may feel angry. When he's angry, *he remembers to take a deep breath and count to five. He tells the other players, "Good game!" No matter what, Daniel Tiger is always a good sport.*

STEP 3: Create a "Power Card." On this card, there will be a picture of your child's superhero along with three important rules to remember to be a good sport. State the rules as directions from the superhero. For example, *Daniel Tiger says, "A good sport always waits his turn."*

STEP 4: Read your child the short script often and have your child read and bring out their "Power Card" before they play a game.

WHY THIS ACTIVITY WORKS
By pairing your child's special interest with appropriate behaviors, they'll be motivated to handle challenges that come their way!

COLOR ME CALM

5 Years – 10 Years

WHAT YOU'LL NEED: a coloring book with peaceful scenes and colored pencils or crayons.

As soon as your child has the fine motor skills to use colored pencils or crayons to color in pages, you can begin to do this activity together. This may be something your child already does with you or at school, but it's also an excellent activity to teach your child to do when they're feeling anxious.

- Keep a coloring book and colored pencils or crayons on hand.
- Encourage your child to describe how they feel during times of coloring that are not related to difficult situations.
- Have discussions with your child to help them understand that certain activities can make them feel calm. Explain that if coloring is a calming activity, they can do it to feel better when they're upset.
- If coloring doesn't draw out soothing descriptive words for your child, explore other similar activities and continue the dialogue. For example, doing a puzzle may be calming for your child.
- Eventually, regardless of whether coloring is a primary tool for your child to calm down, they will begin to understand that they can change their mood by doing certain tasks, and that together you will find out what works.

WHY THIS ACTIVITY WORKS

Coloring is proven to soothe a person during stressful times and to increase feelings of relaxation. In fact, coloring can even lower your child's heart rate and bring them into a meditative and tranquil state. This activity empowers your child to take charge of their mood. Your child may find that coloring is especially calming or may decide to share what they would rather do instead. Either way, they'll begin to assume responsibility for the choices they make and the effect on their body.

TIP For younger children, hold off on conversations about the effectiveness of coloring. Instead, to help them calm down when they begin to show a pattern of increasing anxiety, simply offer them the opportunity to color.

APPLES AND BANANAS

5 Years – 11 Years

This activity will help your child strengthen the cognition skills they need to self-regulate. It also teaches motor planning and includes a lot of fun! The game is similar in concept to the brain teaser task "rub your tummy and pat your head at the same time."

WHAT YOU'LL NEED: two different colored balls, one you'll call "apple" and the other "banana."

THE RULES

- This game can be played with two or more people.
- The apple ball can only be rolled, while the banana ball must only be thrown.
- Sit down together on the floor and keep the balls moving back and forth between you, making sure that the "apple" is rolled, and the "banana" is thrown.
- See how long you can keep the balls moving in the correct motion before someone makes a mistake.
- You may want to begin by just passing one ball at a time while calling out the fruit and motion, such as "apple roll," until your learner gets the hang of it.

WHY THIS ACTIVITY WORKS
Children with autism are often rigid in their thinking. They may be used to doing things the way they originally learned them, and struggle with shifting their mindset to move beyond this. This game practices their flexible thinking and impulse control, while having the added benefit of working on gross motor skills and hand-eye coordination.

TIP Once your child becomes proficient, increase the complexity of this game by adding in a third ball, the "orange," which must only be bounced. Alternatively, if you have more than two players, you may decide that it can only be passed to the right or left.

BEAUTIFUL BUTTERFLY

6 Years – 10 Years

WHAT YOU'LL NEED: a large piece of paper or poster board and crayons, markers, or paints.

Butterfly breathing is an amusing and creative way for your child to practice calming down by shifting the focus of their attention to their breath. Because this breathing exercise is about a beautiful butterfly, it's enjoyable for your child to perform and easy for you both to remember in the moments you need it.

1. Create pictures of beautiful butterflies. Label the butterflies with adjectives that remind you both of being calm, such as "tranquil," "quiet," "serene," "soft," and "peaceful." Hang the poster put on a wall to remind everyone in the house to use their butterfly breathing when they begin to feel stressed or uncomfortable with a situation.

Continued →

2. Teach your child about lungs and how they work to create breath. Say something like, "Inside your body you have lungs. Your lungs have a very important job. They allow you to breathe, and every time you take a breath in, your lungs expand. When you exhale and push your breath out, your lungs shrink again." Have your child rest their hands on their ribs and try to feel their own lungs expanding and shrinking with each breath they take. Once they're able to concentrate on their lungs enough to successfully "find their breath," it's time to show them butterfly breathing.

3. Ask your child to imagine their arms are wings. Together, stand up and spread your wings open wide into a *T* shape. Begin breathing slowly in and out. With each breath in, curl your wings into a circle toward your body. As you slowly exhale, open your wings back out into a wide, stretched *T* shape once again.

4. After your child has done about 10 slow butterfly breaths, ask them if they feel like the butterflies you drew on your poster earlier. Do they feel quieter and more relaxed? It's likely that they do. And it's a good time to explain that they can do butterfly breathing whenever they're upset and it will help them feel calm.

WHY THIS ACTIVITY WORKS

One of the easiest ways for your child to calm down is to stop focusing on the current situation, person, or thing that's causing them to feel stress. This can be accomplished in a variety of ways. One quick and simple method is for your child to shift their focus to their breathing.

TIP Try other fun variations of butterfly breathing by having your child lie on their back or sit on the floor with their legs crossed. Sometimes lying down or sitting will add to the relaxing effect of butterfly breathing.

WHIRLYBIRD

6 Years – 11 Years

WHAT YOU'LL NEED: a square piece of paper.

Does your child love origami? Many children do, and folding paper methodically is a great calming activity. If you've never done origami with your child, you'll likely discover this is one of their favorite activities. You and your child will be creating whirlybirds with a very special purpose—they'll provide a variety of ideas for how to relax during times when anxiety begins to build.

Continued →

Start with square paper.

Fold over into triangle.

Unfold the paper.

Fold over into triangle in the other direction

Unfold the paper.

Fold each corner into the center of the square.

The paper should now look like this.

Flip the paper over.

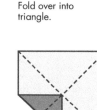

Fold each corner into the center of the square.

The paper should now look like this.

Write a number on each small triangle as shown.

Write calming strategy here.

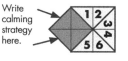

Add your 8 calming strategies by lifting each flap and writing one strategy for each number.

Turn over and write a color on each square.

Fold amd unfold twice, making rectangles in different directions each time.

Insert your thumbs and index fingers into each corner.

Completed Whirlybird.

WHIRLYBIRD, CONTINUED

1. What is an origami whirlybird? A whirlybird, sometimes called a fortune teller or chatterbox, is a piece of paper folded into a shape that can be held on the tips of your fingers and played as a simple children's game.

2. You'll want to add calming strategies to the center of your whirlybird. Examples include: butterfly breathing, draw a picture, take a walk, get a drink of water, ask for a hug, and give a self-hug.

3. Once you've constructed your whirlybird, you can role-play different situations that may cause stress for your child and have them use the whirlybird to choose a calming strategy. Complete the role-play by practicing the calming strategy. Take turns role-playing each calming strategy.

4. Keep the whirlybird with you at all times and hand it to your child when they need to use a calming strategy. If your child is old enough, they can carry the whirlybird.

WHY THIS ACTIVITY WORKS

Once constructed, this whirlybird will be a visual support for your child to use when they're upset. It will provide visual choices of relaxation strategies to use when they're in a stressed state and need to calm down.

CHOOSE YOUR OWN ADVENTURE

6 Years – 11 Years

WHAT YOU'LL NEED: 6 to 10 pages of blank white paper, a stapler, and markers, crayons, or colored pencils.

Creating a "choose your own adventure" story is one way you and your child can explore a variety of ways to calm down. It will be up to you how long the book should be, but keep in mind you'll need more pages than anticipated because this book will have multiple endings.

1. Begin the story by introducing a main character. Invent a problem that makes the main character very upset. Describe what the main character is feeling (for example, anger or sadness) and if their body is overwhelmed by a sensation (for example, from heat, heart racing, or tight muscles).

2. Create a page that gives the reader the following choice: Should the main character use a calming strategy or melt down into disruptive and inappropriate behavior? On this page offer a specific calming strategy as one option and describe what the alternative inappropriate choice looks and sounds like as the second option.

3. Follow each choice with an instruction to turn to a specific page. For example, "If Adam should get under his weighted blanket on his bed until he feels better, turn to page 5. If Alana should drop her body to the floor and scream loudly, turn to page 10."

4. Complete the book by writing pages 5 through 9, describing the calming strategy in more detail, including a happy ending that explains how choosing to use the calming strategy made the main character, their friends, or their family feel better.

5. Use the last page to describe the main character's choice *not* to use a calming strategy. This should be a shorter ending briefly describing the natural consequences. For example, "Alana felt upset for another hour and didn't get to play."

WHY THIS ACTIVITY WORKS

Using social narratives is an evidence-based practice for teaching children with autism ages 6 to 11. After creating and reading through this story multiple times, your child will be able to remember some of their favorite calming strategies and is more likely to use them when needed.

TIP For beginning writers, the book should be short and include only the choice to use or not use one calming strategy. For more advanced writers, the book can be longer and include options for the reader to choose from a variety of calming strategies, giving opportunities to write multiple happy endings.

DON'T STRESS IT

7 Years – 11 Years

WHAT YOU'LL NEED: paper, something to write with, and scissors.

Children with ASD commonly find it difficult to control their emotions and may overreact when faced with an upsetting event. This can interfere with a child's ability to function normally day-to-day. The next activity will help your child recognize what events should create which level of emotion.

For this activity, draw crossing lines on a piece of paper to create four boxes. Label the four boxes with the following emotional states/problem levels, one in each box.

1. **Happy and calm:** minor problem

2. **Disappointed:** little problem

3. **Frustrated:** medium problem

4. **Angry:** big problem

Next, cut small strips of paper and write sample scenarios your child may face, such as:

- cleaning up a mess of toys
- a friend accidently stepping on your toe
- not knowing an answer on your homework assignment
- someone hurt you

See if your child can match the scenario to the emotional state. Discuss what scenarios they should consider a crisis versus those that are no big deal. Further explain how best to handle a problem by doing things such as asking for help or walking away.

WHY THIS ACTIVITY WORKS

Children with ASD may have difficulty managing their emotions, responding appropriately to others, and efficiently maneuvering through everyday life. When they understand what is worth stressing over and what is not and are given the tools to calm themselves, they'll feel much better navigating daily challenges.

TIP This is an intermediate- to advanced-level skill. Make sure your learner has a clear understanding of basic emotional states and can describe what makes them feel different ways before attempting this activity. Adjust the vocabulary to suit your child's comprehension level.

CHAPTER TEN

LET'S LEARN!

Children first learn foundational academic skills, and as they grow, the remainder of the academic knowledge they accumulate builds upon these skills. To learn these vital foundational academic skills, children must also possess pre-academic skills. In Applied Behavior Analysis, pre-academic skills are called "learning-to-learn" skills. Children who have these skills are able to sit still, focus, and follow. Children with autism often do not naturally develop learning-to-learn skills. Many children diagnosed with ASD find it difficult to learn basic academic skills, let alone more advanced concepts, because they don't yet have skills such as sitting still in a chair, paying attention to the teacher, or complying with simple or complex instructions. Other important learning-to-learn skills to teach your child before moving on to academic instruction include waiting, transitioning between activities, and following group instructions—the last being essential for a child to succeed in a school setting.

This chapter includes activities that will help your child become school-ready and increase their learning-to-learn skills while teaching foundational academic skills. If your child doesn't yet have learning-to-learn skills, you'll want to first focus on developing them, by engaging in the first few activities of this chapter. This will help them avoid frustration. When a child does possess the vital learning-to-learn skills, they can easily and enjoyably learn academic skills. You and your child will be surprised by how diverting and entertaining it is to teach and learn academic knowledge with fun activities and games.

BLOCKS VS. SOCKS

2 Years – 6 Years

WHAT YOU'LL NEED: blocks, socks, and other items to sort, two paper plates, and something to write with.

Categorizing is a skill that children typically develop naturally early in life. Matching, sorting, and eventually advanced categorizing of items helps children understand the rules, patterns, and features of items in the world around them. If your child is not yet proficient in this foundational academic skill, you can play this sorting game as a first step.

BEFORE TRYING THIS ACTIVITY

1. Make sure your child has the prerequisite skill of visually discriminating between two items. So, if you have a block and sock out on the table and you ask them to "touch the block" and then "touch the sock," can they do this correctly?

2. Make sure your child can match objects. So, if you have a block and a sock out on the table, and you hand your child another block, will they match it with the block on the table?

3. Practice the skills above with reinforcement and repetition until your child masters them. Once you've established that your child has these prerequisite skills, you can move on to teaching them to categorize using this sorting game.

HOW TO PLAY

- Give your child a pile of blocks and socks mixed together and ask your child to sort them. It's helpful to have your child sort the items onto two paper plates on the table, one labeled "blocks" and the other "socks." This will give them a visual border to help them understand what's expected in the game.
- Once your child has mastered this step, you can further develop this skill by making it more challenging. Try adding a third or fourth item to sort in the mix.
- Then switch to sorting items that are more similar in nature, such as various colored pom-poms or different shaped blocks.

- Eventually, move on to categorizing items by more complex features, such as zoo versus farm animals or kitchen items versus school supplies.
- See if your child can think of their own way of sorting a varied array of items. You can play this game by sorting items by feature (red versus blue), function (things you eat versus things you play with), and classification (vehicles versus clothing).

WHY THIS ACTIVITY WORKS

This activity is a gradual way of introducing your child to the concept of categorization. It will allow them to see items in novel and varied ways. It's a great way to build on the knowledge your child already possesses and further expand it in preparation for future academic tasks like reading and writing.

MIRROR THE QUEEN

3 Years – 6 Years

WHAT YOU'LL NEED: nothing needed for this activity.

This game is designed to practice learning-to-learn skills. The ability to concentrate is a skill your child must possess in order to learn other academic concepts. Having the ability to focus on one thing long enough to watch, wait, imitate, listen, and follow directions is the basis for learning.

This game can be performed virtually anywhere! It's a good game to play while waiting to get your food at a restaurant or for your doctor's appointment to begin. To play, you should sit or stand facing your child at an arm's distance away. You'll start out as the "queen" (or "king") and designate your child as the "mirror." As the queen, you'll make up any silly moves and instruct your child to mimic your actions as though they are your mirror image. So, if the queen lifts her left arm while tickling her own tummy with her right hand, your child would lift their right arm while tickling their own tummy with their left hand. It's a good idea to start with simple, one-move actions, then add to the complexity. Don't forget to give your child a chance to be the queen (or king), too!

WHY THIS ACTIVITY WORKS

This activity will slowly build your child's ability to focus on tasks because it requires extreme concentration for them to accurately mirror your actions. Remember to provide positive reinforcement when they make the right moves!

TIP Holding positions for longer and longer durations is a great opportunity for your child to practice patience, another skill required for success with more challenging academic concepts.

SLAP MATCH

3 Years – 11 Years

WHAT YOU'LL NEED: index cards and markers or colored pens or pencils. Optional: a timer.

Slap Match is an incredibly versatile two-player card game. It can be modified to teach a variety of academics, from colors and shapes to presidents and foreign languages. Kids love it because it's fast-paced. The basic concept of Slap Match is for the main player to run out of cards as quickly as possible. In most cases, you'll be the dealer and your child can be the main player.

1. Use index cards to create a deck of item cards and correlating color cards. For example, if you decide to make a deck of 20 color cards, 10 of the cards will have pictures of a colored item, and the other 10 will be the names of the colors. One card will say "yellow," and the partner card will be a picture of a yellow banana. The next card will say "pink," and the partner card will be a picture of a pink pig, and so on until you have 20 cards total.

2. Separate the deck into two piles. One pile will be for the dealer and the other for the main player. In this example, the dealer (caregiver) will have all the cards with the names of colors and the main player (your child) will have all the cards with the pictures. Cards go facedown in front of the players.

3. The main player will pick up only the top card. In this example, the child picks up a card with a picture of a blue car on it.

4. The dealer will pick up the top card and flip it over face up on the table for 3 to 10 seconds before flipping over the next card and placing it over the previous card as its replacement. In this example, the dealer has first revealed a card that says "yellow" and left it visible to the main player for 5 seconds. The dealer then flips over the next card and replaces the yellow card with a new card that says "blue."

5. The object of the game is for the main player to get rid of all their cards as quickly as possible. They can only put down their card when they see its partner card revealed by the dealer. In this example, as soon as the child sees the caregiver reveal the "blue" card, the child puts down their card with the picture of the blue car and says, "Match!" They've just matched their first card and have only nine more to go. They then select the next card off the top of their pile and attempt to

Continued →

make a match as the dealer quickly cycles through the color card deck.

6. The trick is that *if the main player sees their card's match,* they must put down their card quickly, before the dealer flips over the next card and the opportunity is lost. If the main player is too slow, the same "blue" card will come again later because the dealer will cycle through the cards, over and over, until the main player has matched all their item cards one by one to the dealer's revealed color cards.

7. Setting a timer can increase the excitement of this game. In this case, the main player must match all their cards before the timer dings.

WHY THIS ACTIVITY WORKS

Many children with autism have memorized important facts but cannot quickly retrieve the information when necessary in daily life. This can be because of delays in processing information. Slap Match is specifically designed to increase your child's speed and accuracy with known information, also called fluency. *Fluency allows your child to use what they know to successfully interact with people and the world around them.*

TIP You can create the deck of playing cards to match the academic level of your child. Create the deck to teach multiplication, state capitals, or Spanish vocabulary. (Examples: The "2 x 3" card matches with the "6" card. The "California" card matches with the "Sacramento" card. The "Hello" card matches with the "Hola" card.)

CRAFTING MY NAME

4 Years – 7 Years

WHAT YOU'LL NEED: paper in a variety of colors for cutting; a piece of plain paper; and scissors, glue, and something to write with.

One important academic skill all children need to learn is to recognize, spell, and eventually write their own name. For children with autism, remembering the string of letters that forms their name, especially a long name, may be a daunting task. This is a bright and colorful way for your child to learn to use their name in an academic setting.

1. Cut the colored paper into strips of increasing sizes. The smallest strip should be big enough to write only the first letter of your child's name, the next size larger strip will fit the first two letters, and so on. Use a mix of colors.

2. Put the plain piece of paper in front of your child. Stack the strips down on the table in descending order (largest on the bottom), so the first letter of your child's name is at the top.

3. Have your child pick up the first letter of their name and ask them to glue it to the top of the plain paper. Then ask your child to pick up the next paper with two letters of their name and glue it right below. Every time your child glues down another colored strip

of paper, ask them to read the letters on the strip out loud.

4. Continue this until they've crafted their name in a rainbow of colors.

WHY THIS ACTIVITY WORKS
Remembering a long string of letters or numbers can be difficult for a child with ASD. When the sequence is broken down into small, simple steps, it's less overwhelming and much easier to learn.

TIP To increase the difficulty of this activity, mix up small pieces of paper with one letter of your child's name on each piece. Have your child put them together to form their name. Then, add the component of writing the letters on paper. Start by having your child learn to write the first letter, then the first two. Gradually teach more of the letters at your child's pace. Your child will learn to recognize, spell, and write their name in no time!

FLASH DANCE

4 Years – 11 Years

WHAT YOU'LL NEED: music, a small prize, and a variety of flash cards on any topics your child needs to learn (such as letters, shapes, and colors for younger children, and word definitions, math functions, and presidents for older children).

Facts, facts, facts. How do you teach your child the overwhelming number of facts they need to know for school? Instead of dragging your child to sit at the table so you can drill them with flash cards, here's a way to help them learn in a totally entertaining way.

1. Lay out deck of flash cards on the floor in the shape of a large circle, spreading across as much space as possible.

2. Turn on the music and have your child walk or dance from card to card.

3. When the music stops, they have to answer the question or identify the person, shape, or color on the card they are touching. Have your child turn over the card to see if they're correct. If they are, remove the card from the circle.

4. Your child wins the game when all the cards are gone. Make sure there's a fun prize at the end!

WHY THIS ACTIVITY WORKS

Moving the body, especially movement related to vestibular (inner ear) and cerebellar (brain-stem) stimulation, has positive effects on brain function, likely beacuse of the increased oxygen our brains receive, which strengthens neural connections. Movement as simple as jumping, dancing, or walking briskly can increase your child's ability to remember information and come up with new ideas. Get your child moving and see just how much they can learn and remember!

TIP Create multiples of the flash cards your child has trouble with so they come up repeatedly during the game.

FEEL AND LEARN

5 Years – 8 Years

WHAT YOU'LL NEED: pipe cleaners and small craft supplies like buttons or pompoms. Optional: index cards and glue or a hot glue gun.

In this activity, your child will enjoy the feel of chenille pipe cleaners while learning about letters and numbers.

You can wrap two pipe cleaners together for a longer length or cut the pipe cleaners to a smaller size for easier formation, depending on what will work best for you and your child.

LETTER AND NUMBER FORMATION: You may want to start beginner learners by walking them through, step by step, how to form their favorite letters and numbers with the pipe cleaners. You could also write the letter or number on a piece of paper so your child can do their formation using the paper model as a guide. Use words that will help your child remember the formation—such as "C: big curved line" or "5: line down, hook, cross at the top"—while you have your child trace the letter or number with their finger.

WORD FORMATION: Once they're ready, have your child move on to letter blends and building words formed from the pattern consonant-vowel-consonant, like "cat" and "dog." Alternatively, you can build the words and have your child read them to you.

1:1 CORRESPONDENCE: While forming numbers, bring out the pom-poms or buttons and spend time together matching a quantity of objects to the corresponding pipe cleaner number.

WHY THIS ACTIVITY WORKS
Using pipe cleaners is a great way to give your child a sensory experience while they learn letters and numbers. This kind of tactile learning is essential to cognitive development. Children struggling with academics can improve their long-term performance by using a variety of tactile sensory activities.

TIP Create sensory-friendly flash cards by using a hot glue gun to affix the pipe cleaner letters and numbers onto index cards.

ALL ABOUT HANDWRITING

5 Years – 8 Years

WHAT YOU'LL NEED: a stress ball, clay, tongs, scissors, a pencil gripper, a tray of sand or rice, paper, and something to write with.

Handwriting is a skill with many different components. Hand strength, grip, letter formation, and spacing are all involved in building your child's handwriting proficiency. Here are some easy and effective ways you can help your child improve their penmanship.

HAND STRENGTH: Squeezing a stress ball, clay, or dough is a good way for your child to develop their hand muscles. If your child can squeeze the item 10 times, encourage them to do it 15 times, and so on.

GRIP: Using scissors and using tongs to pick up items and to put together and take apart small building block scan improve your child's grip. A simple rubbery pencil gripper can also make a big difference for your child because it physically guides your child's hand to remain in the proper grip.

LETTER FORMATION: Have your child use their index finger to write letters in a sand or rice tray. This is a fun way for them to practice letter formation while enjoying a sensory experience at the same time. You can also draw squares on a piece of paper and ask your child to write letters inside them. Slowly decrease the size of the squares and watch in amazement as the size of your child's letters

also shrink! If your child tends to raise their wrist or arm while writing, have them write letters on a slant board or use a weighted wristband.

STRUCTURE AND SPACING: To help your child stay within the lines while writing on handwriting paper, highlight the border lines with glue. Be sure to let the glue dry before they write. To teach your child to space individual words in a sentence, start by using a small treat, like a chocolate chip or a mini marshmallow, to hold the space. Then, transition your child to using their finger between words.

WHY THIS ACTIVITY WORKS

Handwriting is an essential life skill for children. It increases their ability to communicate and strengthens their visual perception for reading. The academic arena is often dependent on written formats to demonstrate and share knowledge. Unfortunately, handwriting is frequently difficult for children with ASD to master, as it involves complex motor planning and cognitive aptitude. These exercises and adaptions will make it easier for your child to steadily gain confidence in and mastery of their writing ability.

READING BEYOND DECODING

5 Years – 10 Years

WHAT YOU'LL NEED: a book, paper, and something to write with.

Some children with autism have advanced reading abilities and can even learn to read without any formal training. This is called *hyperlexia*. One characteristic of hyperlexia is a fascination with words. Another is advanced memorization ability, which enables these children to decode and recognize words at a very early age. But children who possess this exceptional ability to read may not fully comprehend what they're reading. Here's an activity that can be used to help your child develop stronger reading comprehension skills.

1. Choose a short book that's about 15 pages long.

2. While reading, define unknown words.

3. Create a list on paper of relevant information, like facts about characters, plot, setting, conflict, and motives. You or your child may write the list.

4. Link the information to your child's prior knowledge. Try to relate what your child is reading to what they've already experienced.

5. After finishing the book and completing the list of relevant facts, have your child write three to five sentences to summarize the book.

6. Review and revise the summary together.

WHY THIS ACTIVITY WORKS
Children with autism are often visual learners, so the written steps in this activity will assist your child in organizing the relevant information from the story and comprehending the meaning of what they've read.

COLORFUL SYNONYMS

6 Years – 11 Years

WHAT YOU'LL NEED: paint sample color cards with 4 to 6 gradual colors per card. (You can pick these up at a hardware, paint, or home-supplies store.)

This activity will expose your child to a broad range of vocabulary, which will in turn expand their language use, develop their understanding of what they've read, and improve the complexity of their writing.

1. Think of a word that your child understands and may be overusing when talking or writing. Ideas of simple word choices include "big," "fun," "happy," and "said." Let's use "big" as our example.

2. Find synonyms for your chosen word. Some synonyms for "big" are "large," "giant," and "enormous."

3. Write the words randomly on a sheet of paper.

4. Explain to your child that these words all have similar definitions but can be ordered according to how strong each word's meaning is.

5. See if your child can help you write the words in order according to intensity on the paint card. So, "big" would be written in the lightest colored rectangle, then "large" in the next darker color, and so on.

6. Try to complete one paint card each day or even one a week.

WHY THIS ACTIVITY WORKS
This activity will benefit your child in multiple ways. The card showing words correlated with gradually darker colors will give your child a visual aid to assist in remembering synonyms for commonly used words. This will improve their understanding of connotations or the deeper meanings behind the words they use when reading or while speaking with another person.

PICTURE THIS

8 Years – 11 Years

WHAT YOU'LL NEED: note cards, blank paper, a timer, and something to write with.

If you and your child enjoy drawing, this is definitely the activity for you. Here are some quick and easy instructions on how to create your own guessing game made from words and pictures! This special game will help your child understand fractions, both by recognition and physical value.

CREATE THE DECK OF PLAYING CARDS

Make about 15 playing cards by writing a fraction and a suggested item on one side of the card, leaving the other side blank. For example, one card will say "1/4 of a pizza" and another will say "3/4 of a window."

PLAY THE GAME

- Decide who will be the artist player and who will be the guessing player.
- Set the deck of playing cards in a pile facedown on the table.
- The artist player picks a card from the top of the deck and doesn't reveal it to the guessing player.
- Set the timer for 30 seconds.
- Once the time begins, the artist player attempts to draw what is on the playing card. If the words "1/3 of an apple" are on their card, they'll only draw 1/3 of the apple and not the whole apple. Use color and details as hints.

- The guessing player will have the remainder of the 30 seconds to guess both the item name and the fraction of the item they're seeing.
- If the guessing player correctly says "1/3 of an apple," they earn a point.
- If the time runs out and they don't guess correctly, the guessing player doesn't earn a point, and it's the other player's turn to guess. Remember to share the correct answer before moving on.
- Trade off being the guessing player and the artist player until all the cards in the deck have been played.
- Once all the cards are gone, the player with the most points is the winner.

Continued →

PICTURE THIS, CONTINUED

WHY THIS ACTIVITY WORKS

For some children, fractions just look like a silly way to write numbers rather than a method of representing the parts or percentage of a whole item. Giving your child the opportunity to see a variety of different fractions with coordinating pictorial visuals gives them the ability to truly understand what fraction numbers symbolize. The added benefit of this game is that it also uses pictures of common household items, which will help your child appreciate that fractions are an important concept to learn and can be used in their daily life.

TIP Adjust the amount of time for each round to fit the needs of your child. Try using more difficult fractions, such as whole numbers with fractions, if your child is learning advanced fractions. If your child is learning to add and subtract fractions, put the name of the item and the equation on the playing card and have them draw the answer to the equation as the item. For example, if the card reads "Banana 3/4 − 1/2," the artist player should draw 1/4 of a banana.

CHAPTER ELEVEN

LET'S BE INDEPENDENT!

Parents want their children to learn how to live independently. For children with ASD, it can be particularly challenging to master the wide variety of self-help tasks required to get through each day. Executing these tasks independently involves memorizing the multiple steps of each one, keeping the steps in the correct order, having the gross and fine motor skills to physically complete the steps, and understanding the safety issues involved in many tasks.

Imagine the wonderful difference it can make in a child's life when they're able to get up in the morning, use the bathroom, get dressed, brush their own teeth, make a simple meal, safely walk to the local marketplace, visit the grocery store, and even make a necessary purchase—all by themselves! ABA programs begin teaching these skills early on and continue for many years as the child grows and matures. The level of independence a child will eventually reach is, of course, unique to that child.

There are many techniques caregivers can use to assist their child in learning daily living skills. Playing games, crafting, and using evidence-based teaching strategies to make learning effortless are all great ways to successfully teach a child to independently engage in the tasks of daily life. This chapter outlines a few of the most practical and fun activities a parent can do at home with their child.

BRUSHY BRUSH BRUSH

1 Year – 3 Years

WHAT YOU'LL NEED: paper, stickers, a few different kinds of toothbrushes and toothpaste, and a special reward.

Brushing teeth, for many children and parents alike, is a dreaded part of the day. Luckily, it doesn't have to be! Here are some tricks to make it much more enjoyable for you and your child.

STICKER CHART

Create a chart with the days of the week listed vertically. Draw two squares below each day of the week, one with a drawing of a sun to represent morning brushings and one with a moon for nighttime brushings. For every brushing you do with your child, give them a sticker in the corresponding square. Decide how many stickers they need to earn before they receive an even bigger reward. If brushing is extremely difficult for your child, you may want to reward them after they earn just two stickers. Sticker charts are a form of *token economy*. They motivate children to practice their best by offering a set number of sticker "tokens" that can be traded in for a highly preferred reward.

THE ART OF DISTRACTION

Sometimes skillful distraction is all parents need to get their kiddos to open up and let them brush. Whether it's singing a silly toothbrushing song for the duration of brushing, having a favorite stuffed animal assist with brushing, or letting toothbrushing be the only time your child can watch a two-minute cartoon, it's all worth it to get those pearly whites clean.

SENSORY SENSITIVITY

Children with autism may actually have sensory issues surrounding toothbrushing. Have your child look at themselves in the mirror to be aware of the sensations they are experiencing. Consider using a flavorless toothpaste or putting just a bit of paste on the brush. Try a brush with extra soft bristles or an electric toothbrush. Your child may need to learn to gradually tolerate more pressure on their teeth and gums over time.

WHY THIS ACTIVITY WORKS

Tooth care is an extremely important daily living skill for a child's health. The strategies in this activity are tried-and-true methods to help your child overcome their aversion to brushing, making the task more tolerable.

CHAINING FOR INDEPENDENCE

2 Years – 11 Years

WHAT YOU'LL NEED: paper and something to write with.

Chaining is a great method to teach just about any daily living task involving multiple steps. Chaining is a way of teaching a complex skill step by step. This activity uses hand washing as an example. You can easily follow the steps below to create a chaining procedure for any self-help task you would like to teach your child.

STEP 1: Write down the list of steps to complete the task. Be sure to perform the task as you write it, as you may be surprised by just how many steps can be forgotten.

1. Turn on the water.

2. Pump soap into your hands.

3. Lather the soap on hands for 20 seconds.

4. Rinse hands in water.

5. Turn off water.

6. Dry hands with towel.

STEP 2: Decide whether you will teach the steps with forward or backward chaining.

BACKWARD CHAINING teaches a complex skill from the end to the beginning. The last step in the chain is taught first. Once the learner has mastered this step, then the second to the last step is taught. The learner masters more and more ending steps until they can complete the entire skill independently. With backward chaining, you would help your child complete the first five steps of hand washing, and then ask them to independently dry their hands. Once your child is able to dry their hands by themselves, you can assist with the first four steps and then ask your child to both turn off the water and dry their hands by themselves.

FORWARD CHAINING teaches a complex skill from the beginning to the end. The first step in the chain is taught initially. Once the learner has mastered this step, then the second step is taught. Each time a new step is taught, the previous steps are completed first, and the new step is added, until the entire skill is acquired. With forward chaining, your child would turn on the water by themselves, and then you would help with the next five steps. Once your child can turn on the water by themselves, you'll ask them to both turn on the water and pump the soap on their hands by themselves and give assistance with the remaining four steps.

Remember to reinforce your child's efforts! The more independent they are, the more praise and rewards they should be given. This will motivate your child to work toward independence, step by step.

WHY THIS ACTIVITY WORKS
Task analysis—breaking a large task down into small, ordered steps—is an evidence-based practice for teaching children with autism and is often a necessary requirement for children with autism to learn a complex, multistep skill.

TIP How do you know which chaining procedure to use? Well, if there are easier steps at the beginning, start there by using forward chaining. Alternatively, if you think your child will feel a great sense of accomplishment by independently completing the last step of the task, use backward chaining. It's up to you.

POTTY PARTY

3 Years – 5 Years

WHAT YOU'LL NEED: underwear and very special rewards. Optional: training pants.

The time will come for your child to potty train, and making this a fun activity for your child is the key to success. Instead of *potty time*, I like to call it a *potty party!* Before using this potty-training plan, you'll want to make sure your child is at least three years old and can independently move their body up and down (as in sitting on and getting off the potty).

STEP 1: LEARN THE STEPS. Familiarize your child with the steps of using the bathroom. Create a small book with the steps by either taking pictures of your child demonstrating each step or finding pictures to print from the internet. Alternatively, you can purchase a book depicting the steps. Talk with your child about the steps while reading the book.

STEP 2: MAKE THE BATHROOM AN ENJOYABLE PLACE. Hang out in the bathroom while you engage in fun activities that your child loves. Read books, watch videos, sing songs, and give tickles and treats.

STEP 3: PROVIDE LOTS OF HYDRATION. Give your child plenty to drink throughout the day, while keeping them in underwear. Use a diaper only at night, if necessary. If you have to run out of the house during this process, consider putting your child in training pants over their underwear so they'll still feel the wetness if there's an accident.

STEP 4: SET YOUR TIMER AND REINFORCE SITTING. Have an alarm sound every 15 or 30 minutes. When it sounds, take your child to sit on the toilet. Reinforce them just for sitting even if they don't go.

STEP 5: REWARD SUCCESS. *This is crucial*—make sure the reward for success is highly valuable and reserved only for use during potty training. Your child gets this special reward only when they successfully use the toilet.

STEP 6: DON'T MAKE A BIG DEAL IF THERE'S AN ACCIDENT. Just repeat steps 4 and 5 and your child will begin to notice there are no rewards for accidents and big rewards for success.

WHY THIS ACTIVITY WORKS

This activity will increase your child's toileting skills because almost all the steps involve pairing positive reinforcement with learning a new self-help skill, which can be a nonpreferred task. Pairing with reinforcement is very effective in teaching new skills to children with autism. Creating a positive experience around the bathroom routine can make all the difference in toilet training a child with autism. It may take a bit longer to plan a terrific toileting experience for your child, but it will be well worth the time and energy to achieve this goal.

TIP Try to pair reinforcement when teaching a variety of other skills to your child, such as learning a new household chore, doing homework, playing with a new friend, or taking a bath. You'll likely transform the experience into one that's much easier and more enjoyable for you and your child!

GRIP IT RINGS

3 Years – 8 Years

WHAT YOU'LL NEED: an exercise band tied into a circle or an old T-shirt cut into three-inch strips; a hair band, scrunchie, or jelly bracelet; and a die.

This activity provides practice with the motions of dressing, while working on developing your child's strength to accomplish the task.

SHIRTS AND PANTS

Tie the exercise band or shirt strips to fit your child's body size. Have your child use this stretchy circle to strengthen the motions of dressing. For practice putting on a shirt, have your child put the circle over their head, then their arms through, and then pull it down to their waist. For practice putting on pants, have your child put their legs through and then pull the circle up to their waist. Additionally, have your child use the circle to rehearse the motions of undressing.

SOCKS

Have your child practice gripping and stretching the band by putting it on their feet up to the ankle and then taking it back off again.

Turn these simple exercises into a game by using lots of stretch circles and scrunchies and a die. Then, trade off rolling the die to find out how many stretchy circles must be put on or taken off during each turn.

WHY THIS ACTIVITY WORKS

The thickness of these items acts as a grip for children to hold on to, making it easier for your child to practice these motor skills while also strengthening their hands. Pretty soon, performing the real task of dressing will feel so much easier!

TIP Make these activities easier with hand-over-hand prompting, or by helping your child complete the task halfway and then having them do the rest independently. You can challenge your child even more by having them use the opposite hand to cross the midline while performing the action or try to put on the rings with their eyes closed.

BUTTON WORM

4 Years – 7 Years

WHAT YOU'LL NEED: a button, fabric ribbon, needle and thread, pieces of felt fabric, and scissors.

Your child will have a blast increasing their independence with this zany and creative project. This is an activity for buttoning beginners and will help your child master how to button in no time.

HOW TO MAKE A BUTTON WORM

STEP 1: Sew the button to one end of the ribbon. You'll want to use a large button (about the size of a quarter) for younger children and a small button (about the size of a dime) for older children.

STEP 2: Tie a large knot at the opposite end of the ribbon.

STEP 3: Cut your felt fabric into a variety of shapes and sizes, averaging three by three inches, so you have room to fit the button through the center.

STEP 4: Fold each piece of felt in half and cut a very small slit in the middle, just big enough for your button to slide through.

Your child will now be able to create a button worm! They can pick up one piece of felt and push the button through the small slit in the middle. Then, they'll pull the felt piece all the way down to the knot.

Have your child do this for each piece of felt to create a colorful felt worm they can give as a gift or put on display.

WHY THIS ACTIVITY WORKS
This is a creative way to make buttoning more fun. It's also easier than buttoning real clothing, as the felt is more pliable. This project will give your child lots of fun as it prepares them for success with the motor movements of buttoning and will gear them up to practice buttoning their clothing.

LET'S GO SHOPPING

4 Years – 7 Years

WHAT YOU'LL NEED: paper and something to write with. Optional: images and a special treat.

The skills involved with successfully navigating the grocery store are necessary for kids tagging along with parents on shopping trips and for their future lives as independent adults. The following tips will make these outings more enjoyable for everyone.

INVOLVE YOUR CHILD IN PLANNING A MEAL THEY ENJOY. With your child, create a list they can take to the store of all the ingredients they need for the special meal. Let your child know they're responsible for finding everything on their list and placing it in the shopping cart at the store.

REFRESH YOUR CHILD ON THE RULES OF BEHAVIOR. When you arrive at the store, before stepping inside, review the rules verbally, with a written social script, or in picture form. The rules could include holding on to the cart at all times, not touching items on the shelves unless they're on the special list, and keeping a calm body at all times. Front-loading your child with what you expect can help tremendously.

CATCH YOUR CHILD BEING GOOD. As you're shopping, remember to consistently praise your child when they follow the rules. If shopping is an especially difficult task for your child, you may even decide to give them small bites of a favorite treat if they're doing well.

KEEP TRACK OF TIME. Get what's needed and head home, especially when you can feel your child beginning to lose patience. If a meltdown occurs, follow through with completing your shopping trip. This lets your child know that acting out won't get them what they want, decreasing the likelihood of negative behavior in the future.

If the shopping trip is a great success, give your child lots of reinforcement for a job well done!

WHY THIS ACTIVITY WORKS
When your child learns to tolerate, and then eventually enjoy, community outings, your family will have the freedom to do more things together. Proactive strategies and positive reinforcement are keys to making this possible.

TIP If your child often exhibits problem behavior in public, it may feel uncomfortable and embarrassing. Consider making small informative cards you can pass out to lookyloos, explaining in just a few words that your child has autism and requesting their patience. Examples can be found online by searching for "autism awareness card."

BANK ON IT

5 Years – 9 Years

WHAT YOU'LL NEED: paper; something to write with; three clear, clean containers; and something to label them with.

It's never too early to begin teaching your child about money management. This is an essential life skill they'll eventually need to gain financial independence. Here are some ideas to think about when it comes to navigating the financial arena with your child with ASD.

Create a short list of chores your child can complete to earn money. Each week, when they finish all the chores, give them a small allowance ($2 to $10).

Label the three containers "Spend," "Save," and "Share." When your child receives their allowance each week, have them put a portion of their earnings in each jar. The money in the Spend jar can be used to purchase small treats and toys. The money in the Save jar won't be touched and may be transferred to a savings account after the jar is full. The money in the Share jar is for a donation to help someone in the community. Have your child choose which charity or cause they'd like to give the money to. Your child will be able see how funds can "grow" and "shrink," which will help them learn the value of money.

WHY THIS ACTIVITY WORKS

Direct practice with actual money is the best way to teach this valuable life skill. When your child understands how to count money and balance a bank account, they have learned an important skill that they will use throughout their entire lifetime. When they understand the value of money, they have learned how to save and accumulate wealth!

RECYCLE RACES

5 Years – 9 Years

WHAT YOU'LL NEED: four Hula-Hoops, four signs ("trash," "plastic," "aluminum," "paper"), a timer, and a large pile of relatively clean garbage. Alternative materials: plain paper, construction paper, and something to draw with.

Learning how to be a good global citizen starts at home and can begin at a very young age. Once your child knows how to sort items, they're ready to begin to assist the family in their recycling efforts.

1. Spread out the Hula-Hoops in opposite corners of your backyard. If you don't have a backyard, skip to step 4. Place one sign inside each hoop. Put one piece of example garbage in each hoop to show your child what's expected. Make sure the examples follow the definition of each type of waste where you live.

2. Each player then gets an equal pile of garbage to use during their turn to race. When it's your child's turn, they'll distribute their garbage into the correct hoops as quickly as possible. Use a timer to keep track of how fast they distribute the items. Keep the clock running even if you have to swiftly correct any mistakes in the sorting.

3. Each player gets a turn to distribute their pile as speedily as possible, and the player with the shortest total time wins.

4. If you'd rather play this game inside, use small pieces of paper with drawings or words, with each small paper representing one item of garbage. Then use large pieces of construction paper labeled with the four categories, instead of Hula-Hoops. With these simple changes, you'll be able to play this game at a table right in your home.

WHY THIS ACTIVITY WORKS

This game will teach your child the correct categorization of garbage needed to recycle and strengthen their fluency with this skill. Fluency is an important dimension of almost every skill your child learns, as it's a measure of speed and accuracy.

TIP If your child is playing this game alone, allow them to repeat the turns as many times as they like to try to beat their own best time.

SAFETY SIGNS

6 Years – 11 Years

WHAT YOU'LL NEED: index cards and printed images, or something to write and draw with.

Safety signs are everywhere, and each one communicates an important message. Often, children don't automatically understand these signs. Take the time to teach your child the meaning of the important safety signs they frequently encounter.

SAFETY SIGN GAMES

Create a deck of playing cards using index cards with images of the signs you're teaching to your child. Make multiple index cards for each sign you're teaching. Print these images from your computer and glue them to the cards, or simply draw the signs yourself. Consider including common street signs, pedestrian crossing, exit, do not enter, danger, restroom, construction, and general prohibition signs. Once you've made your deck of cards, use them to play one of your family's favorite games, such as "Go Fish," "Memory," or "Bingo." During game play, integrate naming the safety signs and teaching the meaning of each.

FUNCTIONAL PRETEND PLAY

After you demonstrate and practice the meaning of each sign, use the signs during playtime. With your child, engage in pretend play using dolls, stuffed animals, and toy vehicles and have them enact what the safety signs tell them to do. This way your child can display their knowledge and learn what the appropriate reaction should be for each sign.

COMMUNITY OUTINGS

Once your child has mastered safety signs during play, take them into the community for real-world exposure to following the safety signs they've learned with you at home. This can be incorporated into outings involving driving in the car, walking down the street, or running errands at stores.

WHY THIS ACTIVITY WORKS

These activities give your child the repetitive rehearsal needed to memorize the meaning of each sign. From direct instruction to play to real-world practice out in the community, your child will gain the exposure they need to react appropriately to safety signs.

TIP Consider using some of these signs in your home. For example, once your child understands the meaning of a stop sign, post an image of a stop sign on your front door to remind your child not to open it. Place a danger sign where hazardous cleaning products are kept, and prohibition signs to indicate no TV watching or that room entry is not allowed.

TIME TO LEARN

6 Years – 11 Years

WHAT YOU'LL NEED: 20 small squares of paper or 20 note cards and something to write and draw with. Optional: small prizes.

At around age six or seven, children typically begin to learn how to read a clock and tell time. This is a valuable skill for children to use in navigating the tasks of the day and completing everything in a timely manner. This activity is a fun memory game that will help your child learn to tell time.

On each of 10 note cards or paper squares, draw a clock with hands depicting a different time of day. On the other 10 note cards, show the same times in a digital format.

RULES OF THE GAME:

1. Put all cards facedown on a table so the times aren't visible.

2. Mix all the cards so they're in no particular order, and then arrange them in straight rows and columns.

3. The first player turns over two cards, revealing the images on the other side. If the two cards show the same time (clock hands and digital), the player wins the pair of cards and continues their turn by pulling two more cards.

4. If the player chooses two cards that don't match, their turn is over.

5. The players take turns choosing cards until all the cards on the table are gone.

6. Players then add up the number of pairs they won, and the player with the most matching pairs wins.

WHY THIS ACTIVITY WORKS

Repetition with reinforcement is a winning combination when it comes to teaching your child a new skill. This game incorporates both.

TIP Make this game more enjoyable for all players by promising each player a small prize for each matching pair they find, regardless of who wins the game. For example, if your child finds four pairs of matching cards, they win four dimes.

RESOURCES FOR PARENTS

BOOKS

Anger Management Workbook for Kids: 50 Fun Activities to Help Children Stay Calm and Make Better Choices When They Feel Mad by Samantha Snowden, MA, and Andrew Hill, PhD, 2018.

Positive Parenting for Autism: Powerful Strategies to Help Your Child Overcome Challenges and Thrive by Victoria M. Boone, MA, BCBA, 2018.

Social Skills Activities for Kids: 50 Fun Exercises for Making Friends, Talking and Listening, and Understanding Social Rules by Natasha Daniels, LCSW, 2019.

ORGANIZATIONS

Autism Speaks is the largest autism advocacy organization in the United States.

autismspeaks.org

Center for Autism and Related Disorders is the world's largest autism treatment provider, offering a variety of resources necessary to help individuals with autism reach their full potential.

centerforautism.com

Autism Beacon was started by a parent of a child with autism and strives to supply the best resources for autism treatments.

autismbeacon.com

WEBSITES

Autism Live is a free resource for the autism community and the world at large.

autism-live.com

Autism Partnership offers detailed video demonstrations illustrating the progression of programming at various stages of skill development.

autismpartnership.com/program-booklets-dvd

Autism Therapy Career College offers online parent education in Applied Behavior Analysis (ABA) through high-quality audio and visual video lessons.

autism-parent-training.com

Different Roads was founded by a mother of a child with autism; it helps other families by handpicking the best autism intervention products available and offering them in one place.

difflearn.com

Kids Yoga Stories offers resources to assist parents teaching their child yoga poses, which help children develop awareness of their bodies and how they move.

kidsyogastories.com

National Autism Resources is an online store for educational toys, flash cards, equipment, and sensory products for autism and special-needs kids and adults, offering more than 1,000 autism products for families, teachers, occupational therapists, speech-language pathologists, and BCBAs.

nationalautismresources.com

REFERENCES

Barbera, Mary, and Tracy Rasmussen. *The Verbal Behavior Approach: How to Teach Children with Autism and Related Disorders*. London: Jessica Kingsley Publishers, 2007.

Carsley, Dana, Nancy L. Heath, and Sophia Fajnerova. "Effectiveness of a Classroom Mindfulness Coloring Activity for Test Anxiety in Children." *Journal of Applied School Psychology* 31, no. 3 (2015): 239–255.

Cooper, John O., Timothy E. Heron, and William L. Heward. *Applied Behavior Analysis*. 2nd ed. Upper Saddle River, NJ: Pearson Prentice Hall, 2006.

Granpeesheh, Doreen, Jonathan Tarbox, Adel C. Najdowski, and Julie Kornack. *Evidence-Based Treatment for Children with Autism*. Waltham, MA: Academic Press, 2014.

Mueller, Michael M., and Ajamu Nkosi. *The BIG Book of ABA Programs*. Marietta, GA: Stimulus Publications, 2010.

Reichow, Brian, Peter Doehring, Domenic V. Cicchetti, and Fred R. Volkmar, eds. *Evidence-Based Practices and Treatments for Children with Autism*. New York City, NY: Springer Science, 2011.

Sundberg, Mark L., and James W. Partington. *Teaching Language to Children with Autism or Other Developmental Disabilities*. Danville, CA: Behavior Analysts, Inc., 2010.

Wodka, Ericka L., Pamela Mathy, and Luther Kalb. "Predictors of Phrase and Fluent Speech in Children with Autism and Severe Language Delay." *Pediatrics* 131, no. 4 (2013): e1128–e1134.

INDEX

ACKNOWLEDGMENTS

This book would not exist if it were not for one of my oldest and dearest friends, Lori Ayin, MEd, RBT, who not only introduced me to the wonderful opportunity to provide ABA therapy to children with autism, but has also worked side by side with me throughout my entire career. She is a rare and special friend, a magnificent mother of two beautiful girls, a talented college professor, and an exceptional scholar and teacher of the science of Applied Behavior Analysis. I cannot thank her enough for her spiritual, emotional, and intellectual support of every contribution I have made to the field of ABA intervention thus far, including this book.

Moreover, in addition to being blessed with the wonderful parents mentioned in the dedication of this book, I have also had the good fortune to be surrounded by many other encouraging and caring friends and family members who have helped me and supported me through each and every step of my life's journey. I could not be more thankful for the good and kind people in my life whose presence has gifted me with the ability to write this book.

ABOUT THE AUTHOR

KATIE COOK, MED, BCBA, graduated with honors from California State University, Long Beach. Katie continued her education at National University, La Jolla, and earned her Master of Education with a Specialization in Autism. She later studied under Jose Martinez-Diaz, PhD, BCBA-D, associate dean, professor, and head of the School of Behavior Analysis at the Florida Institute of Technology.

She has dedicated her professional career to building strategies that bring entire families into the therapeutic environment for children with autism. Parent education and caregiver involvement are her passions, and she believes these are the cornerstones of successful ABA programs. Katie is guided by her love for ABA and has spent years building her home therapy practice, *ABA Services*, into a wholehearted organization, characterized by her commitment to helping children with autism. Katie is also the owner and academic director of *Autism Therapy Career College*, an online training institution that offers parent education resources, Registered Behavior Technician (RBT) credentialing services, and remote fieldwork supervision for graduate students seeking their Board Certified Behavior Analyst (BCBA) certification with the Behavior Analyst Certification Board (BACB).

CPSIA information can be obtained
at www.ICGtesting.com
Printed in the USA
LVHW070551220223
739936LV00004B/10

9 781646 114801